MW01029160

Sitting
with God.

A Journey to Your True Self Through Centering Prayer

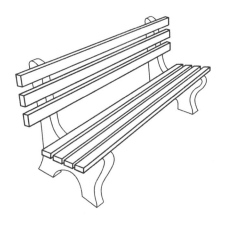

Rich Lewis has given us a book that leads us into the heart and healing of centering prayer. Rich speaks carefully and humbly about his spiritual journey and what he has discovered. He offers readers a gracious introduction and invitation to partake in this soulful practice that will deepen their faith lives.

—J. Brent Bill, author of *Holy Silence*

This book is for both the beginner and those who want to go deeper in both knowing and experiencing Jesus. Lewis will show you the way.

—Nicholas Amato, author of *Living in God*

Rich Lewis's book is a beautiful account of one man's path into the richness of God-centered meditative prayer. This also makes it a most accessible and thoughtful invitation to others to take that same journey. Sprinkled with insightful quotes from other writers, Lewis, in an unusually thoughtful and loving way, makes an attractive, practical case for accessing the presence of God not only in prayer but in all facets of life. Highly recommended.

—Paul Smith, author of *Is Your God Big Enough? Close Enough? You Enough?*

This is a wonderful book! Informative and encouraging, practical and profound, Rich Lewis's writing is earnest, clear, direct, humble, and winsome—more like a letter from a helpful and knowledgeable friend than a dry textbook. Whether you are new to contemplative spirituality or have been at it for a while and seek to deepen your practice, this book will inspire you.

   —Daniel P. Coleman, author of *Presence and Process*

This is a book for those of us who seek a deeper, more spiritual relationship with the Divine, free from the tyranny of words. Widely and deeply read, Rich Lewis writes a simple text that is enriched with wonderful quotes from some of the most inspirational thinkers of our time, so that every page is a revelation. In his quiet, unassuming way, Lewis shares his own experiences and shows us how we too can journey to the silent heart of God.

   —Rebecca de Saintonge, author of *One Yellow Door*

This book is a testimony to the transforming power of God's love working through the regular practice of centering prayer. In this book, Rich Lewis shares generously of his own journey to centering prayer and the difference it makes in his life. His love of God and the spiritual life is contagious, and is sure to encourage the reader to set aside time each day to let God be God through the practice of centering prayer.

—Dr. Philip St. Romain, author of *Reflecting on the Serenity Prayer*

I first met Rich Lewis when he was a senior at the University of Pittsburgh. It has been a joy reading how centering prayer has helped Rich transform his relationship with God, with others and with himself. I encourage you to read Rich's book and begin to experience the transforming power of centering prayer in your own life!

—Rev. Dr. Deborah Winters, Associate Professor of Old Testament, Palmer Theological Seminary of Eastern University

We are a people in search of meaning. But it is a rare person who plumbs the depths of life to find it. Rich is one such soul. Herein lies a courageous invitation to find God and in so doing, find yourself. I wish more people would turn to contemplative practice as Rich has done. It's people like him who light our way.

—Phileena Heuertz, author of *Mindful Silence*

Sitting with God

A Journey to Your True Self Through Centering Prayer

· ·

RICH LEWIS

ANAMCHARA
BOOKS

ANAMCHARA BOOKS
Vestal, New York 13850
www.AnamcharaBooks.com

Paperback ISBN: 978-1-62524-647-9
Ebook ISBN: 978-1-62524-648-6

Cover design by Ellyn Sanna.
Cover image by Victoria Shibut (Dreamstime.com).
Interior layout and illustration by Micaela Grace.

Author's Note: *I intentionally use male and female pronouns
for God interchangeably because God is beyond such limiting
designations. And I consistently gravitate to feminine pronouns,
especially when it comes to writing about prayer.*

• •

Dedicated to my wife,
Trina Lewis, and our three
wonderful children:
Benjamin, Gabriella, & Joshua.

• •

Modern western culture,
especially in America,
has done its best
to keep these two figures,
the Jesus of history and
the Jesus of faith,
from ever meeting.

—N.T. Wright[1]

As we move toward the center,
our own being and the divine being
become more and more
mysteriously interwoven.

—Cynthia Bourgeault[2]

In the deepest forms of prayer . . .
we experience the absolute
or nondual aspect
of Jesus (Jesus' Divinity).
When we return from prayer
we experience the relative
or dualistic aspect of Jesus
once again (Jesus' humanity).

—Amos Smith[3]

The Word became flesh
and lived among us.

—John 1:14

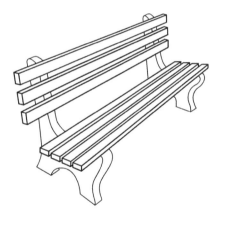

Contents

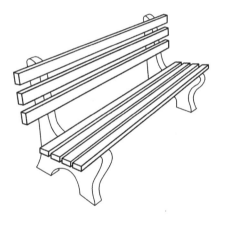

Foreword

CARL J. ARICO

R ich Lewis does not let us settle for an ordinary way of looking at prayer or Jesus.

The power of prayer, properly understood, opens the door to the Mystery of God. Prayer is best seen as a relationship that touches all the levels of a dynamic relationship.

I often challenge couples to look at their love for one another as a glimpse into our relationship with God—a union, and with time, a unity between one another. Their relationships move from acquaintanceship, to friendliness, to friendship, to union, and if they surrender more to one another in the Holy Spirit, into unity. Each level feeds on the other.

In our Christian tradition, levels of relationship intimacy manifest in types of prayer—vocal prayer, meditation, affective prayer, and contemplation (simply put, to read, to reflect, to respond and to rest). The challenge is that we have been taught how to read, reflect, and respond in a compulsory way, but we have not been taught how to truly rest in life or in prayer (Matthew 11:28).

Rich introduces centering prayer as a prayer of resting in God's presence and consenting to God's action—the desire to be in union with God. The image I like is allowing Jesus to wash our feet (John 13:1–17). Before beginning Rich's book, I invite you to read the Gospel of John as he shares the events of the Last Supper. It is a celebration of union and unity, especially as they break bread together—they become companions on the journey (John 13:1–14:7).

The name *Jesus Christ* opens us to a fuller awareness of him. It is a good reminder that we are not dealing with another outstanding human being, healer, miracle worker, teacher, founder of a religion, social worker, or champion of the marginal, but the Son of God, true God and true human. *Christ* has been here from the beginning of time and even before time. *Jesus* was the name he was given when he became human in the fullness of time.

John's Gospel states: "In the beginning was the Word and the Word was with God, and the Word was God" (John 1:1). If we believe this, it means when there was nothing—no-thing—Christ was there. He loved God, and God loved him, and in that dynamic of love came the Holy

Spirit. Their circular dance created and sustained the world as we know it—and as we are still getting to know it, to the point of being one with it, not separate from it. So God has been a living relationship from the beginning. And whatever exists has the presence of God because God is existence. Nothing can exist without God.

"All things came into being through him, and without him not one thing came into being. What has come into being in him was life, and the life was the light of all people. The light shines in the darkness, and the darkness did not overcome it" (John 1:3–5).

Now the awesome revelation: "The Word became flesh and lived among us . . . full of grace and truth" (John 1:14).

The good news is that this Word did not just live among us in the past tense. The living Word is available to us in the present moment when we pray. It also nudges us throughout the day. This is the good news of Rich's book: that the Word is a dynamic presence that was not only experienced long ago, but can be experienced today in the context of a normal life.

Rich Lewis reveals the wisdom of the mystics for our contemporary world—that we can experience Union with God in Christ here and now. When the story of salvation unfolded, in the beginning there was the sense that humankind was separate from God—that we had to earn God's love. But with the coming of Jesus, our eyes and hearts can be opened to see that there is no separation from God in Christ. We can experience not only Union, but Unity, unity with the Divine, so we can say, "It is no longer I who live, but Christ who lives in me" (Galatians 2:20), and "your body is a temple of the Holy Spirit" (1 Corinthians 6:19).

As Saint Ignatius of Loyola prayed:

O Christ Jesus, when all is darkness and we feel our weakness and helplessness, give us the sense of Your Presence, Your Love and Your Strength. Help us to have perfect trust in Your protecting love and strengthening power, so that nothing may frighten or worry us, for, living close to You, we shall see Your Hand, Your Purpose, Your Will through all things. Amen

Foreword

AMOS SMITH

R ich and I have worked together on Recovering Christianity's Mystic Roots (RCMR5.org) since 2014. In our work there has been synergy beyond what could have materialized individually.

RCMR5 has expanded into a social network. Most of this is Rich's doing. He is a natural at reaching out and finding ways to mutually enrich contemplative ministries. Rich has also branched out with SilenceTeaches.com, an engaging website that draws contributors and followers from all over the contemplative Christian map.

Rich and I are brothers on the walk, each with our particular angle and gifts. We have much in common, including love for family, a rooted faith, and a dedication to contemplative Christianity. I realized early on that Rich's passion was centering prayer. And I noticed that as his practice deepened, so did his presence. Rich will tell you that as a result of his centering prayer he is more solid and joyful and that this has shown up in his job and family life. These are not mere words. They are reflected in the lines in his face and the light behind his eyes.

What I admire about Rich's writing is its simplicity and absence of pretense. Whereas I can go off on philosophical tangents, Rich keeps his two feet on the ground. Rich's grounded and sincere delivery makes him readily accessible. He builds the scaffolding from point A to point B. His sentences are short and to the point. He is nothing if not honest, especially about his passion for centering prayer. And his passion is rooted in his experience of God's Real Presence[4] through prayer.

I like how Rich adapts his centering prayer to his busy life as a husband, parent, and employee of a large corporation. For example, he found that his "relaxed efficiency" at work improved when on his lunch break, he went to his car in the parking lot and did centering prayer there. He came back refreshed and more efficient. "Relaxed efficiency" is a wonderful phrase that holds the creative tension between the demands of a corporate work environment (efficiency) and the fruits of committed centering prayer (profound relaxation). This kind of synergy and integration are the hope for twenty-first-century contemplative arts.

For Rich, there is no hyper-image consciousness. There is no deliberation about perception management. Rich simply shows up and speaks his truth, which is disarming and refreshing. For today more than ever we need two qualities in our leaders: first, to show up and second, to speak their truth. We are all called to speak the truth that only we can speak. In this book, Rich speaks his unique truth, which has the potential to restore vivid awareness of God's real presence and action within and to heal our nervous systems. Centering prayer is not just cerebral. It is a holistic healing art that releases decades of accumulated chronic stress encamped in tense muscles throughout the body.

Some criticisms I have heard about centering prayer in recent years are that it is for academics, the upper classes, or monks and cloistered folk. The fact that Rich is a normal middle-class family man, who goes to a normal job in a cubicle for a large company, counters this. Centering prayer is no more relegated to elite cliques than is running or playing guitar. It is a profound and ancient art form available to anyone with the discipline to try and keep trying.

Years ago, I observed Rich's gifts of brevity and truth-telling. I also observed how the Jesus Paradox, as conceived in the minds of the Alexandrian mystics,[5] took a hold of his prayer life and imagination. Now, years later, these gifts have turned into a book. And this book is what I hoped it would be—writing not intended for a preselected group, but aimed at a normal slice of Americana.

Twenty-first-century Christianity needs a viable anchor that is not given to the polarizing extremes of its left and right wings. And Rich Lewis is an apt navigator, grounding his sentences in personal experience and his reverence for "that of God in everyone."[6] If there is anyone who can see past reductionist labels and pigeon-holing to our underlying humanity, it is Rich Lewis.

There have been times on my journey when I needed a grounded word of inspiration, and Rich delivered it with agility and precision. I hope this book does the same for you.

In addition to reading the book, communicate with Rich online. You will notice on his website SilenceTeaches.com that there are many opportunities for continuing education, including centering-prayer resources, newsletters, and the opportunity for one-on-one centering-prayer coaching. And you will find Rich accessible. Miraculously, he has shed the one-step-removed and aloof diseases of our times.

Most of all, I hope you give centering prayer a dedicated try. In other words, I hope you commit to at least thirty consecutive days of centering prayer, slowly increasing the disciplined silences to twenty minutes. As Rich reiterates throughout the book, the regular practice of centering prayer will surprise and transform you.

God in Christ (Colossians 3:3) has called Rich and me to relay the life-giving wonders of centering prayer. And let's be clear, neither Rich nor I are special. We simply show up daily to the chair and the cushion. Like good musicians, every day we practice our scales. Some days we may curse the chair before we sit. That's all part of the long-term journey. Practicing scales, so to speak, day in and day out, nothing more, nothing less—that is what we are called to do.

We are drawn to the primordial silent melodies. They bathe us in ancient waters of calm and of natural great peace. And we hear Jesus whisper through our relaxed minds and nervous systems: "Come to me, all you who are weary and are carrying heavy burdens, and I will give you rest" (Matthew 11:28). And that deep rest is why we keep coming back, rain or shine, year in and year out. That deep restorative and transformative rest[7] is exactly what our hassled twenty-first-century minds and bodies need most.

As I write this foreword in 2020, the United States is reeling from the Covid-19 pandemic. This pandemic has convinced me that centering prayer is what we need more than the talking heads. Covid-19 has convinced us all of the profound uncertainty of our times. The wild fires in California, the pandemic, the consistent aberrant storms scientifically tied to climate change—these phantoms have either swept through our abodes leaving death and destruction or we have narrowly escaped. Either way, now more than ever we need stable people, people who have learned how to quiet their minds.

Just one family member, who knows serenity and composure when hell is unleashed, can make the difference. Someone steeped in disciplined silences can make the difference between the survival and eventual prosperity of family and community members on the one hand, and implosion and self-destructive angst on the other.

Our prayer life and presence make Christianity real and relevant in our fretful over-caffeinated multitasking times. It is an accomplishment to balance the fears, demanding pace, and technology of our times with silence and stillness. May we live into the depth and compelling truth of balance, and may deep-seated balance set us on a path to abundant life (John 10:10).

Our presence is our most integrated and compelling gospel witness. May we be contemplative witnesses to our families and communities.[8] That witness may not necessarily dazzle. Most often, to survive and thrive and to know balance and peace is enough.

Introduction

I came that they may have life,
and have it abundantly.

—John 10:10

In 2013, I began to dabble in silent prayer, a term that's often used as synonymous with centering prayer. I had heard and read that silence can transform you. I wanted to experience this transformation too.

I would force myself to sit in silence. I began to test how long I could sit there. I started with one minute and increased it to three and even four minutes. It was difficult!

Silence and silent prayer are counter-cultural. They are very challenging to cultivate because everything in our culture seems to point in another direction. Yet, surprisingly, it is in silence that I have found profound transformation. And that is the motivation for writing this book. I want to share what I have discovered. The point of this book is to share my centering-prayer sojourn with you. My hope is that my journey will help you with your journey.

Centering prayer is not a race. It is a long-term marathon. Centering prayer practiced daily, monthly, yearly will transform you. It does not replace other forms of prayer; it complements them.

Centering prayer has changed my life and the way I think. It has been so life-giving that I cannot keep it to myself. I have to share it.

–Rich Lewis

PART ONE

. . . .

The Life
of Prayer

Jesus would withdraw to
deserted places and pray.

—Luke 5:16

Chapter 1

. . . .

BEGINNER'S MIND

. . . .

Contemplative Prayer is the world
in which God can do anything.
To move into that realm
is the greatest adventure.
It is to be open to the Infinite
and hence infinite possibilities.

—Thomas Keating[9]

Without unscripted time,
we will never learn to hear the voice of God
because we will be too busy
with our plans and ideas.

—Ian VanHeusen[10]

I cannot imagine a better start to each day than a silent sit.

Silence is not empty. It is filled with God.

When I practice centering prayer, I respond to the invitation to sit with God (Revelation 3:21). When I center like Jesus, I say, "Not what I want, but what you want" (Mark 14:36). I sit in silence to be loved and healed by God. Silence creates a space for me to heal. The space created by silence and stillness helps me find my equilibrium, my center of gravity.

I sit in silence because it is a safe place to let go of my anger—and my guilt for this anger. I sit in silence to let go of jealousy, which is an obstacle to the release of my God-given potential. I sit in silence to let the Creator create through me, to let go and trust God. I sit in silence because I love God. I sit in silence to enter a journey that God and I travel together. Silence teaches me how to live.

Silence is not often thought of as a teacher. Most often our society refers to silence as "dead time." What, if anything, can be special about silence? This is where a transformation has taken place in my life. I have come to see how precious silence is, how silence is God's first language. As Thomas Keating and a number other mystics before and since have stated, "Silence is God's first language and everything else is a poor translation."[11]

Words do not always need to be said. In contemplative prayer we float in the ocean of God. You can't sink because God will hold you. Thomas Keating wrote, "Contemplative prayer is the world in which God can do anything." Our job is to enter and see what happens. We maintain a "beginner's mind"—an openness that allows all our expectations to drop away. As Zen teacher Shunryu Suzuki wrote: "In the beginner's mind there are many possibilities. In the experts mind there are few."[12]

The heart of centering prayer is "consent"—consent to the presence and action of God in our lives. That is it! We do not need to make it complicated. Like the myriad contemplatives before us, we open to the presence of God in silence. We let God do the work. When we center, we let God take action within (Luke 17:21). If we open to God, God will become present, and when ready, God will act within. And we will take this action into our non-centering times of the day.

In a radio interview, Amos Smith mentioned that he has chosen his well and will dig there (as opposed to digging in several wells [traditions]). I feel the same way. I have chosen my well. It is centering prayer, and here I will dig. The silence of centering prayer is not escape from this world but rather prepares me to engage and fully live in this world. The deep well of centering prayer provides a foundation, which gives me the stability and solidity to carry out my life mission.

A Personal and Unique Journey

Centering prayer is a personal and unique journey. We each start where we are and enter the Mystery. When we center, we let go of all preconceived notions. We let God be God. We cannot define God; when we try to do so, we end up with something dead and unhealthy, an idol (Exodus 20:4)! We can only open to God.

We best understand God when we try not to understand God. This goes back to having a beginner's mind. We maintain a posture of openness. We let go and admit that we don't know. We simply trust. We leave our "small mind" and enter the "larger mind." We die to our self. Cynthia Bourgeault wrote, "Dying to self means being willing to let go of what I want (or think I want) in order to create space for God to direct, lead, and guide me into a truer way of being."[13] We die to what the world tells us we need. When I practice centering prayer I move from "let go" to "let be." I let myself "be" with God.

Love is a word that is tossed around a lot in our society. Mystics of old, like Maximos the Confessor, saw the Love experienced in prayer as the highest Love—as a holy state of the soul, which values knowledge of God above all created things. We can't remain in this Love as long as we are attached to anything worldly.[14] I must let go if I want to behold this Love. I let go of all things that engage my senses: sights, sounds, smells, tastes, in order to open myself to God who is ultimately beyond the senses.

The hope of contemplatives, often realized in the lives of saints both ancient and post-modern, is that just as meditation has transformed us, it will transform our society. This is why we show up every day. Centering prayer is the foundation, the context, for everything we do. Centering prayer is powerful. It changes us. The change in us gives birth to change in the world. We could not keep the revitalization of our souls to ourselves if we wanted to. We have to do something with the new found vigor. In God's time, what has transformed us cannot help but transform our relationships.

Centering prayer is powerful, but it is not a sprint. It's a marathon. If we are faithful to our practice, our practice will be faithful to us. Our work is to show up each day—to show up two to three times per day, in fact—and sit with the Mystery we call God. Our job is to sit with God and let God work in us. Each time we sit is another opportunity for God in Christ to take action within us. God will loosen our minds and keep the doors of our minds open.

When people try centering prayer for the first time, I encourage them to simply pray daily as long as they can for thirty consecutive days, and mark it on the calendar. Sits will be five minutes some days and others ten. The point is to simply begin where you are and do as much as you can. Silence is hard to get used to. Give yourself time.

As our bodies need rest, our minds need solitude and stillness. Our minds need to relax, to drop into our hearts and rest with God who is within. It is a pilgrimage from our mind to heart.

My First Sit

On workdays, my first centering-prayer sit is at 5:45 a.m. I always feel some anxiety after I wake. Then I retreat to the basement, light a candle, and sit on a couch. It wakes me up. The anxiety fades. It fills me with interior peace and energizes me for the day.

I use the Contemplative Outreach phone app.[15] The timer is set for twenty minutes. I read the opening prayer. I have selected, "Open my heart to Your love." That is all I want to do. I want to forget me and open my heart to God's love.

During centering prayer, I begin by detaching from my thoughts and emotions. In my mind I silently say, "I let them go to You." I think about my upcoming day. I think about what worries me and makes me anxious. I think about areas where I need mental and physical healing. I think about others who I am worried about. I think about my anger, frustration, hurt. As the thoughts arise I let them all go to God. This process heals my mental, physical, and spiritual being.

I might go through my "let-go" process for about one minute. Then I am done. If I have more thoughts after that, I mentally visualize my sacred icon as my intention to open to God's presence and action within. I internally visualize the icon for no more than one second. (I will say more about the icon later.)

My goal then is to forget me, to let go. My goal is to sit in the presence of Mystery—to remove barriers to God. My goal is to let God gaze directly on me. The only way God can do this is if I let go of me and my baggage.

Anthony de Mello wrote,

Words cannot give you reality. They only point, they only indicate. You use them as pointers to get to reality. But once you get there, your concepts are useless. A Hindu priest once had a dispute with a philosopher who claimed that the final barrier to God was the word "God," the concept of God.[16]

Words can get me started but I must let go of them if I want to find God, or more precisely let God find me. I am in a posture of openness and consent to the action of God. As soon as I have any thoughts, I let them go. I enter the spaces between my thoughts. Here God in Christ finds me.

God is not my thoughts. God is beyond my thoughts. My thoughts only limit God. Many mystics have exclaimed in one form or another that the most profound knowledge of God is to know God as unknowable.[17] I enter centering prayer with this posture of openness and unknowing. Whenever thoughts, emotions, and day planning begin, I mentally visualize my Jesus icon to bring me back. Sometimes I do not have to visualize the icon. My thoughts float away on their own.

After twenty minutes, the three consecutive tones of the closing bell ring. When the third and final bell has rung and there is silence, my sit is over. I know I did not fall asleep. I describe it as a place I go. I have let go. I do not feel anything. It is a vacuum. I have merged or fallen into something larger than me. When the closing bell rings I re-emerge from this place that I will call Divine Union. I now feel joy and peace. I am grounded and excited to begin my day.

Letting go during centering prayer is meant to continue the rest of your day. What do I mean by this? I mean we should never hold on to thoughts and emotions that are not productive. They stop us from accomplishing the daily tasks that we need to complete. When I become worried, I let it go. When I become anxious, I let it go. When I become frustrated, I let it go. When I become afraid, I let it go. It is okay to acknowledge emotions but they will often stop us dead in our tracks. We need to let them go so we can move on. I realize that at times there are thoughts and emotions that we need to deal with. I do not suggest repression. I suggest that we let them go so we can move on with our day. Later in the day if we need to deal with them, we can.

When it comes to thoughts, there are two extremes. We can clutch the thought like clutching a rock (attachment)—or we can hurl the rock away from us (aversion). Centering prayer is about simply letting the rock rest in the palm of our hands, then gently tilting our hand so it drops. It is a gentle movement, void of tense reactivity.

Gently letting go is a reflex. The more we do it, the stronger the reflex becomes. At first we will hold on to an emotional tangent for a day or more. Then, with practice, the tangent only takes half the day. Then, in time, as we become more skilled at the art of letting go, we can let go of the tangent after ten minutes.

My Second Sit

Never underestimate the power of an afternoon prayer sit. Don't skip it. Even if you do not feel like it, do it anyway. A second sit refills your reservoir. It helps you finish your day.

I work in an office. In the early afternoon I stop what I do and walk to my car. It is usually anywhere between two and four p.m. It does not matter how busy I am. I need this time. My aisle mates know where I go (I have shared my practice with them). I sit in the driver's seat of my car. Dependent upon the weather, I crack the window. Here I take my second sit. I am always amazed by how productive the rest of my day is after this second sit. It refreshes me. I need it! Often my reservoir is empty or runs on reserves. It needs to be refilled. I am amazed at how much better I feel after this sit.

After each sit, I experience various feelings. I am calm, at peace, excited, energized. I am ready to continue the day. During centering prayer, I completely let go and plunge into the depths of God in Christ (Colossians 3:3). I no longer skim the surface.

I am on a journey. I want to be engulfed by God's presence, power, and glory. The only way I can do this is to let go. I don't really know what God will do now that God has my full consent. I want to be in God's Presence. I want to be in God, and I want God to do whatever God wants. I consent. This is exciting. What God in Christ does with me will be revealed in the fruits of my actions during my non-centering parts of the day.

· · · · · · · · · · · · · · · · · · · ·

Questions for Reflection and Discussion

1. What, if anything, can be special about silence? What can silence teach us?

2. What does it mean that God is beyond thoughts and emotions?

3. When we pray, do we always need to talk? What if we are silent? How does this make you feel?

4. What does it mean to rest in God?

Chapter 2

. . . .

THE REAL WORK OF CENTERING PRAYER

. . . .

God just is—without any limitation.
And the way to connect
with this "Is-ness" is to just be, too.

—Thomas Keating[18]

When engaged in contemplation,
we rest in God resting in us.
We are at home in God at home in us.

—James Finley[19]

Centering prayer leads to contemplative prayer. Contemplative prayer is union with God—rest in God.[20]

Centering prayer is simple:

1. Show up.
2. Let go.
3. Open your heart.

God will do the rest. During centering prayer we leave our "small mind" and enter a "larger Mind."

These centering prayer guidelines are pulled from the Contemplative Outreach website:[21]

1. Choose a sacred word as the symbol of your intention to consent to God's presence and action within.

2. Sitting comfortably and with eyes closed, settle briefly and silently introduce the sacred word as the symbol of your consent to God's presence and action within.

3. When engaged with your thoughts, return ever so gently to the sacred word.

4. At the end of the prayer period, remain in silence with eyes closed for a couple of minutes.

As you begin and continue your centering prayer, keep in mind that thoughts and silence both have a role to play. The content of some thoughts expresses what needs to be healed, and silence creates the space for healing to take place.

Trust the Silence

When I center, I let go and trust the silence. Letting go comes first, and then comes trust. I don't know what will happen next. I let go of expectations. I let myself be vulnerable. I do not know what feelings and emotions I will experience both during and after my sit. I trust that God is in charge and knows what is best. Centering prayer is a continuous practice of trust in God who waits in the fertile silence.

Centering prayer teaches us to let go. We even let go of repressed and painful thoughts and emotions. Centering prayer lets God heal our body, mind, and soul. Centering prayer lets God work in us.

God can fill us with whatever She feels we need. We might be filled with love, peace, or mental and physical healing. We might be filled with sudden needed knowledge to accomplish our daily tasks or with an urge to serve. We might be moved to make a major shift in our personal and work life or nudged to try something new. We might be asked to make a call to repair an estranged relationship or sit and listen to someone in pain who needs a hug and an attentive ear.

When we incorporate silence into our day, the day is transformed. Silence is a time when we let go and let God work in us. Why is it so important to "let go"? Thomas Merton wrote, "Only when we are able to 'let go' of everything within us, all desire to see, to know, to taste, and to experience the presence of God, do we truly become able to experience that presence with the overwhelming conviction and reality that revolutionizes our entire inner life."[22] This is what we do each time we "let go" during centering prayer.

"Letting go" during silent prayer is merely practice for "letting go" that must continue during our daily lives. We need this continuity if we truly want to see, live, and experience abundant life (John 10:10). We let go of our pet project and check in with our spouse about her hard day. We set aside our all-consuming online work to start the cherished nerf-gun battle with our eight-year-old son. We let go of our exciting plans for the day and visit our friend struggling with sobriety.

Centering Prayer Connects Our Divinity and Humanity

Jesus is "at once both human and God."[23] It is a beautiful paradox. And we too are both human and divine.

We are not God. However, we possess an inner divinity at our core (Genesis 1:27). Let's call it our little "d." We are most human when we let go and act from our inner divinity. Centering prayer connects the dots within us and creates a unified picture. During centering prayer we let go of our humanity. We enter into rest in God. We connect our inner divinity, the little "d" with the Big "D." Our divinity and God's Divinity become one. We enter Divine Union.

During the non-centering parts of the day, our little "d" yearns for expression. It is best expressed when we allow ourselves to be fully human. It is a wonderful mystery. We are fully human when we are fully divine. We can celebrate and honor both aspects of our nature. We can let them work together in a dynamic unity.

We see the paradoxical humanity and Divinity at work in the life of Jesus throughout the Gospels. For example, at one turn Jesus curses a fig tree, which is what I might do on a bad day. Then a few moments later He heals someone (Mark 11). When we connect with Jesus' paradoxical Divinity and humanity, we are more likely to discover and mirror that same paradox at work within us.

If we can put together the contradictions of humanity and Divinity at work in Jesus, we are more likely to put the two together within ourselves. We are messy broken humans and we are made in God's image and destined for glory. Both are true. The deeper we plumb one truth, the more deeply we recognize and honor the other.

Let God Love You

When we are filled with God's peace and love, we know everything will be okay. And yet, during centering prayer, we even let go of God's love and peace. They are simply thoughts and feelings that block us from the full power and glory of God that shines upon us and within us in stillness and silence.

When we completely let go, we experience that we are utterly loved by God. Our whole being is filled with God in Christ. When God fills us, we experience what we need. When I say what we need, I mean what God knows is best for us. We feel and experience these things during our non-centering times of the day too. For example, this book was a centering-prayer experience. Every day, I let go. I let God fill and show me what He wanted me to place on the book's pages.[24]

Rebirth

Silence is God's classroom. I return to it each day and let God teach me.

Often our lives can become boring. We get into routines and do the same things from morning till the time we retire at night. Centering prayer teaches us to let go of the old ways we do things. We let go of our routines and open to new experiences. I am a routine person. What will happen if I alter my routine? I will birth a new experience.

This book is a rebirth. Before this book I did not write anything longer than ten to fifteen pages. This book was birthed out of my relationship with Amos Smith. I came across his book, *Healing the Divide: Recovering Christianity's Mystic Roots*, while I browsed Amazon. I decided to obtain a Kindle free sample. I did this when it was first published in 2013. I was not ready to read it, so I set it aside.

I came back to *Healing the Divide* in January of 2014. I read the sample and liked it. It resonated with me. I purchased and read the full Kindle version once, then went back and read it again. I checked out Amos's website. I found his site's contact page and began to ask Amos questions about centering prayer and inner divinity, what Amos referred to as our little "d." We continued an email dialogue. At the time, I led a prayer group at my church. I told him about this group and he offered to Skype into one of our meetings to talk about centering prayer, silence, his experiences, and his book. I took him up on it.

A few months later, Amos asked if I wanted to help him with social media. I began to tweet for RCMR5.org (Recovering Christianity's Mystic Roots) in May of 2014. My tweets became a part of my centering-prayer routine. I center first thing in the morning. Following my centering prayer session, I tweet quotes and articles that resonate with the RCMR5 key themes. RCMR5 themes are centering prayer, new monasticism, Christian mysticism, the Jesus Paradox, and nonviolence.

The tweets have become a part of my morning prayer time. I begin with centering prayer, move into verbal prayer, followed by tweets, and end by reading a few pages in the book I'm currently reading. Then, I begin my day. I need these forty-five minutes in the morning with God. I love this routine. It makes me whole, prepares me for the day.

In June of 2014, Amos inquired if I might consider writing a book about centering prayer and the Jesus Paradox (at once Divine and human), which are dear to me. Amos liked my approach to teaching centering prayer and thought that what he termed my "accessible style" would benefit others.

Until the idea developed in conversation a book was the furthest thing from my mind. The first thing I did was discuss it with my wife. I have a full-time job and a family with three children. Writing a book would involve an enormous time commitment. Together, we decided that I should write the book. We agreed that once a week, I would slip away for two to three hours and write. (Since then, I have managed to slip away twice per week). I also wrote early in the morning while the family sleeps. I did not want to impact the time I spent with my family. And luckily, I don't require many hours of sleep.

What I am getting around to is this: centering prayer plowed the field and prepared the soil. It opened me to try something totally new and different. Centering prayer cultivates an inner freedom; it makes us more able to let go and more open to try something new. This freedom is akin to the beginner's mind that we mentioned in chapter 1.

Rebirth Two

I love to read. I enjoy all kinds of books related to centering prayer, contemplative prayer, and the Bible. On my one-hour drive to and from work I often listen to podcasts that interview current authors, such as Richard Rohr, Cynthia Bourgeault, Derek Flood, Brian Zahnd, N. T. Wright, Rob Bell, Peter Enns, John Dominic Crossan, and Amy Jill Levine. I enjoy their diverse and compelling perspectives.

I enjoy talking and listening to people, but it's sometimes hard for me to naturally connect with others. Despite that, I decided I wanted to share with others the perspectives I was reading, so I started a biweekly adult faith exploration class at my church. I decided that the class structure would be: listen to a thirty-minute audio and let the class react to what they heard. I advertised it on the church Facebook page and in a weekly email to all members. And people came!

I provide this as an example of a rebirth because I simply decided to let go. I am not a biblical scholar nor a speaker. Who am I to think I can teach topics on Sundays to other adults? But I realized I do not need to teach. I can let the audios teach for me. All I have to do is let the attendees listen and react, and then facilitate and ask questions. It worked. It was fun.

If it hadn't been for centering prayer, I would not have taken on this project. I would have had too much resistance to it, and I would not have had the courage to let go and take the plunge.

Rebirth Three

I am an introvert and the last thing I want to do is stand up in front of my church congregation and speak or teach.

The pastor asked me to do just that. He asked me to lead the congregation through a centering-prayer exercise as part of the service. I agreed. I created an overhead that discussed the four centering-prayer guidelines.

I shared that I center twice per day: once in the morning to start my day and in the afternoon or evening after dinner. I mentioned that I also often do a spur-of-the-moment center at any point in the day. I explained that I have centered in my backyard, on car rides (when I am a passenger), in parking lots when early for appointments, or at two or three in the morning if I can't sleep.

I then told everyone we will do this together. I explained that I use the Contemplative Outreach App that is on both my iPhone and iPad. I set the timer. The entire congregation centered with me. It was powerful.

I have also shared my practice with co-workers in my work aisle. They enjoy hearing about it.

The point is that I push my comfort zone now more than I have in the past because I can get past my aversion to public speaking, teaching, book writing. Likewise, I can let go of my attachment to pet projects and jump to the aid of a family member or whatever action the moment demands. In other words, I experience more freedom now. My mind is more like a beginner with many possibilities, open to what reveals itself in the moment, open to something new.

Centering prayer is a daily spiritual practice of emptying and rebirth.

The Door

The Beloved says from the other side of the door, "Open the door and come in, so we can experience just how One we might become."[25] Centering prayer is the door I open to come in and experience oneness with God.

I searched for this door for thirty years. In the process, I knocked on many doors. For now, I will not knock on any new doors. I walked through the centering-prayer door and have decided to stay in this house. It resonates with me. When I center, I feel like I walk into God's house. I drop off all of my excess baggage at the front door. I sit in God's living room. God has a special chair for me. I am invited to sit and rest. It is here that I am loved, healed. It is my special time with God. No words need to be said. We are two friends who need each other (James 2:23). I need God's love and healing during centering prayer; God needs my action in the world during my non-centering times of the day.

Centering prayer will continue to be the door I open to experience oneness with God. I always feel welcome in God's house. I will also share this door with as many people as I can. They can then determine if this is the right door for them.

Centering prayer grounds me so I can better perform in this world. Centering prayer opens my eyes. I now see the Divine where I previously did not. Centering prayer opens me to the continuous presence of God. It counters the dullness of my routines and encourages me to let go, take risks, and try new things.

God Prays in Us
(1 Thessalonians 5:17)

We enter silence not to pray but to have God pray in us.

We die to self and to who we think we are. We are not fathers, mothers, sisters, brothers, friends. We are not our occupations, the daily tasks that we perform, or our accomplishments. We are not our to-do list. Nor are we our opinions, our agenda, or the compliments and criticisms we harbor. We are not the sense of self-worth we feel when we get a raise, receive a bonus, or receive lavish praise and compliments from others. We are not our feelings that may include anger, jealously, joy, pride, loneliness, and depression.

We enter silence to empty ourselves of all those things. We enter silence to rest in the arms of Infinite Love. We enter silence to trust this Infinite Love. When we self-empty, we allow the Holy Spirit to fill us. We let the breath of God breathe within us. We let God pray within our depths. God works at such a deep level that we are unaware it happens.

I dare not define what it is that God prays in me. It is a mystery that is up to God alone. My job is to self-empty so I can be filled with God. When we are asked to lose all, to be emptied out, we are filled with the fullness of God in Christ. Basil Pennington stated, "Lord, I believe that you are truly present in me, at the center of my being, bringing me forth in your love."[26]

When I enter silence and self-empty, I open to God at the center of my being. I let God pray in me. Then I let God bring me forth in infinite love.

Letting Be

David Frenette stated, "As centering prayer deepens, letting go yields to letting be—being in God's being."[27] When I enter the spaces between my thoughts, I experience God's Being.

I do not know I have entered Divine Union until my session is over. Sometimes when the closing centering-prayer bell rings, I do not know where I have been. Then I realize I am "being in God's being." I have lost track of time. I have lost my sense of me as I entered oneness with God. If this is what death is like, I have nothing to fear. Divine union is a rest in pure love. No words need to be said because it is a place that transcends words. No thoughts or emotions need to be felt. Our being is in God's Being. We rest in pure love.

When we enter into the depths of centering prayer, we take a mini-vacation from ourselves, our anxieties, our hang-ups. We experience something inexpressible and holy. Just as we come back from a vacation renewed and invigorated, likewise we emerge from centering prayer with a beginner's mind that is revived and ready for whatever may come next.

. . . .

Questions for Reflection and Discussion

1. When is the best time for you to practice silence? How can silence prepare you to start your day?

2. Where can you practice centering prayer? How can you carve out time during your day for one or two sits per day?

3. Does silence scare you? What kinds of thoughts and emotions come up while you sit in silence?

4. How does just being with God in silence help you to just be with life?

Chapter 3

. . . .

GOING DEEPER WITH CENTERING PRAYER

. . . .

Prayer means the shedding of thoughts.

—**Evagrios**[28]

In essence, contemplative prayer
is simply a wordless,
trusting opening of self
to the divine presence.

—**Cynthia Bourgeault**[29]

In Matthew, Mark, and Luke, Jesus asks the question, "Who do you say I am?" (Mark 8:29). Jesus answers this question for us through the practice of centering prayer. Jesus speaks to us in the silence.

Centering Prayer Teaches Us Who Jesus Is

In centering prayer, rather than search the Gospels and let them reveal the answer, we let Jesus come directly to us in the silence. We let go. We open ourselves. We let the Christ Light or "Seed of Christ" within be revealed and act within us.[30] We let ourselves be filled with the work that God wants us to do. God reveals answers to long-term questions, prompts us to do new things, and asks us to serve in new ways. The silence of centering prayer reveals Jesus' imprint on our souls. This imprint is hidden like a seed in the ground and the water of centering prayer reveals it and makes it grow.

Through centering prayer, we begin to mirror Jesus. The small tree begins to look like the big tree—it has the same imprint. We become the human actions of Jesus. We become His hands and feet in the world, the Body of Christ. Centering prayer connects us to Jesus, and then we go forth into the world. We prove that Jesus is not dead, for He is alive through our actions. We are His body at work in the world.

Centering prayer connects us to Life, reminding us who we are as it teaches us how to live. We are the loving and compassionate actions of Jesus in this world. We participate in the larger mystical mind and heart of Christ who said "before Abraham was, I am" (John 8:58).

Some contemplatives have commented that there are two great sacraments of the church—the sacrament of Holy Communion and the sacrament of silence. When we take Holy Communion, we participate in the Body of Christ—and when we practice disciplined silences, we also commune with Christ. Holy Communion is both symbolic and substantial, while the sacrament of silence is mystical and subtle.

Two Angles on Jesus

There are two approaches to Jesus. I have been writing about the Jesus of experience—His Presence that we experience in prayer, and I think most intimately in silent prayer. Then there is the Jesus of knowledge—what we know about Jesus intellectually through reading the New Testament, studying the historical Jesus, and so on. Both are important; the Jesus of faith and of experience on the one hand, and the Jesus of history and knowledge on the other. In this book I write about both aspects, which for me form a seamless whole.

Thirst for Silence

I believe there is a great thirst for silence in our world. I teach centering prayer at churches in the Philadelphia, Pennsylvania, area, and people come, wanting to learn more. They ask, "Is there another way to pray? How does it work? Why should I try it? How can it help me?"

Why do people yearn for silence? After all, silence seems impossible to achieve. There are always noises around us. In our homes we hear the sounds of the air conditioner or heater. The dishwasher, washing machine, and dryer run; clocks tick; television and radio send their voices out into the air. Many people say they need white noise in the background. Some people cannot fall asleep without the television.

I believe the thirst for silence is not a longing for the absence of sound. Instead, it is a thirst for inner stillness, a thirst to stop the incessant interior thoughts and commentaries. This interior dialogue repeats things like this: "I am not loved.

I am not confident. I am not good enough. I could have done a better job. I am not happy. I am bored. I am afraid to try new things. Don't pick me, I can't do this. I am jealous." We desperately want to stop this dialogue. We want to hear a different Voice, the Voice that says, "I love you. You can be confident. You are good enough. You do a great job. I am all you need to be happy. You no longer need to feel bored. I have new plans for you."

I am not just writing here about positive self-talk, although that can be highly beneficial. What I'm describing is a connection with a deep-down profound affirmation of the substance of our being. We are hardwired for intimacy with God, and when we find it, we naturally come to embody a deeply rooted confidence, stability, and positivity.

God waits for us in the silence, so we don't need to fear it. In the depths of silence God will speak to us. Silence teaches us who we are. We can trust the silence.

A silent-prayer practice such as centering prayer is one path that can help us hear the Voice of God in Christ. Christian meditation[31] and prayer labyrinths can also help us hear. There are many contemplative paths that will open us to God's Voice. Each person will need to find the one or more paths that work best for their individual circumstances. My path is centering prayer sprinkled with lectio divina[32] and photography. You'll need to find your own unique path.

God's Wonderful Work

In centering prayer we let go of all thoughts, emotions, and bodily sensations. Next we trust the silence. We don't know what will happen when we become silent. We simply let go and still our racing thoughts and emotions.

During centering prayer, we allow ourselves to be vulnerable. We do not know what feelings and emotions we will experience during and after our sit. We need to remember that our job is simply to trust God. We need to let God be in charge. We need to trust that God knows what is best. God is in the silence. He loves us beyond what we can comprehend.

What will God do once we let go and trust? She will fill us with whatever She feels we need. We might be filled with love, peace, or mental and physical healing. We might be filled with sudden needed knowledge to accomplish our daily tasks. We might be inspired to serve. We might be challenged to make a major change in our personal or work life.

It is vital to incorporate silence into our daily life because this is where the magic happens. When we let go and trust God, God can begin to work in us. We begin to surprise our family and colleagues with a new repertoire of thoughts, words, and deeds. We are better able to recognize when our spouse does not want our opinion but instead needs a hug and a listening ear. We notice a colleague at work is struggling with a task, and we step in and help her to complete her assigned duties.

Basil Pennington wrote, "In Centering Prayer we go beyond thought and image, beyond the senses and the rational mind, to that center of our being where God is working a wonderful work."[33]

Life Is a Prayer

James Finley wrote, "Even now by faith we lose our footing and fall into a new, unending center in which we are upheld by God and not by the narrow base of our ego's self-assertion."[34] The silence of centering prayer teaches me how to lose my footing—and be caught by God. It enables me to let go of my ego's insistence that it is the center of the world.

Silent prayer is a paradox. We both freefall into an infinite Mystery and are upheld by God at the same time. The deeper we fall, we never hit bottom, for God has no limit. We plunge into the depths of Mystery, yet we are held securely by the love of God.

Faith is what allows me to take this leap into the unknown. What do I have faith in? I have faith that there is something much bigger than me. I do not have to live in separation. Instead, I can live in this Mystery; I can participate in it, rest in it. I am safe inside it, unconditionally loved.

Centering prayer is a safe place to practice life in God so that we can continue to live in God during our non-centering times. All of life can become a beautiful prayer that abides with us throughout the day and its many activities.

A Personal Example of Centering Prayer's Power

As I wrote this book, my father passed away. My first centering-prayer session after his death was very powerful. I will never forget it.

The morning after he passed, I turned on my prayer app on my iPad. The opening bell chimed and I began. I immediately began to cry.

I visualized my sacred icon. I cried again.

Again, I visualized the icon. Again, I cried. I do not recall how many times I repeated this cycle. Each time I cried, I let go more deeply as

I consented to God's presence. Eventually, the tears stopped, and I was at peace.

Then I let go of the peace. I just was. I was in the spaces between my thoughts. I was with God and God was with me. True peace, even in the midst of my grief! The closing bell chimed, and I returned to my life, strengthened. I still grieved my father, but now I had let him go, knowing that he was in God's hands. This was the most powerful centering prayer session I have ever experienced.

Centering prayer teaches us to strengthen the reflex of letting go, which is a wonderful training for life. As we stop compulsively holding on to thoughts during prayer, we build the spiritual "muscle" that allows us to let go even of the people and things in our lives that we love most. We give it all to God— thoughts, worries, loved ones, and all.

To Pray Is to Embrace All That God Loves

William Meninger, one of the founders of the centering-prayer movement, stated the following in an interview:

As you embrace God, you are embracing everything God loves. What does God love?

God loves everything God has created. Everything. Now this means that God's love extends to the outmost bounds of an infinite cosmos that we can't even fathom, and God loves every tiny atom of that because He created it.[35]

When I sit in centering prayer, I unconsciously pray for all God's Creation. I do not realize I do this. If I did, it would be mind-boggling. But imagine the power of a silent sit in community with others. Together, we pray for all Creation. Together, we love all God's creation. Together we feel the love of a great family reaching back generations and forward to generations unborn. This extended family includes all our relations, who share our DNA, and it also includes four-leggeds, creepy-crawlies, and mountain ferns, and even the trace metals from stars that course through our circulatory system.

• • • • • • • • • • • • • • • • • • • •

Questions for Reflection and Discussion

1. Do you need white noise in order to sleep or do things?

2. Do you have the thirst for silence?

3. Do you believe God loves you? Why or why not?

4. Are you afraid of the silence? Why or why not?

5. The author states that God prays in us during the silence of centering prayer. Have you ever experienced something like this? If so, what actions has God prayed through you?

Chapter 4

. . . .

THE FRUITS
OF CENTERING
PRAYER

. . . .

The fruit of the Spirit is love, joy,
peace, patience, kindness, generosity,
faithfulness, gentleness and self-control.
There is no law against such things.

—Galatians 5:22–23

The contemplative Christian classic *The Cloud of Unknowing* teaches, "Lift your heart up to the Lord with a gentle stirring of love, desiring him for his own sake and not for his gifts."[36]

We enter centering prayer with no expectations. We enter to receive the gift of contemplative prayer, in which we experience God's presence within. It is just God and us. Our whole being, body, mind, and soul, marinates in the Mystery. It is a prayer of love without ulterior motives. We pray because we love God. That is our only motivation.

This means I do not enter centering prayer for the fruits. During centering prayer I let go of expectations, and by doing so, I create a space for God to move. I say, "Here I am God. Do with me whatever you want" (Luke 22:42). When I let go, anything can happen. God can act within me in whatever way She chooses. Each time I sit with God is another opportunity for God to act. God also acts within me during my non-centering times.

David Frenette said, "You learn to float in God in prayer in order to swim with God in life."[37] During my non-centering times, I swim with God in life and notice what God has prayed in me. Others notice what God has prayed in me. I discover that God has given me a gift. I experience the side effects of centering prayer—the fruits.

When I started centering prayer God said, "Rich, slow down! I want you to see the things that you previously overlooked." Contemplative life is about being willing to slow down enough to see the marvels of life at work all around us. The speed of our affluent technological society is daunting. Slowing down through centering prayer helps us counteract the incessant speed. It helps us reconnect with simple pleasures and the wonders of our younger years.

That is one of the fruits of centering prayer that I've experienced. There are others.

Friends Share with Me

One way we can tell we are being transformed is if other people find us more available, more attentive. The more the barriers come down in our time of sitting still before the Lord, the more we can welcome people.[38] This has happened to me as a result of centering prayer.

Since I started centering prayer, I have noticed that friends seem to be more open. They allow themselves to be more vulnerable when they are with me. They talk more openly to me about challenges in their lives. They share personal affronts and trials in their family life and career. They speak about issues they have repressed but can now discuss.

On my good days, God gives me the gift of presence and space, in which I can more deeply listen. Now, because of centering prayer, I know how to listen. I know how to connect. I know when to ask a question. There is now a space that previously did not exist. When I sit with a friend, we both enter this space, where we can both let go. We are free to talk and to pause to listen. It is a safe space.

I have noticed that people at church, folks I don't know well, will come up and talk to me. They have heard me share about centering prayer, and now they seem comfortable with me. They ask, "How are you, how are your children?" On my good days, I have the gift of inviting presence. I would not be given this beautiful gift if it wasn't for centering prayer. I do not ask for this gift. It is just given to me.

Centering Prayer Seeds

Others see what centering prayer has done for me and are curious. This is another fruit of my practice. My practice plants seeds in others.

For example, my daughter recently approached me. She knows I practice centering prayer in the morning and evening, and she knows that my place to sit is on a basement couch. She came downstairs and said, "Teach me." My daughter has attention-deficit disorder. It is difficult for her to sit still and quiet; she needs to talk. But I taught my daughter the steps.

I told her that first I sit with my eyes closed. When my thoughts drift, I mentally visualize my Jesus icon. She explained that she did not want to center with her eyes closed because she was afraid she would fall asleep. I told her that the sacred glance might work well for her instead. The sacred glance is done with the eyes open. During centering prayer she focuses on an object or space on the floor three to five feet in front of her.[39]

The first time we did a one-minute sit. We have now worked up to a ten-minute sit. After each sit ,we spend time together and talk. This is our special time together to sit with God. I am grateful for this time, which is remarkable given her disorder. Experts such as Dr. Andrew Weil and many others have advocated the benefits of meditation for optimal health, and I am certain that centering prayer has had a positive impact on my daughter's disorder.

I have also shared my practice with the people in my work aisle. They know that in the mid-afternoon I leave my desk and sit in my car. They know that meditation is important to me. I recently shared my practice with one of my work peers who wanted to learn more. At church as well, I have shared my experience and why it is important to me. As a result, I now know a widening circle of people who practice centering prayer. And in the past year, I have started phone consultations with a growing number of clients who are interested in developing a centering-prayer practice.

When people see how this practice has transformed my life, they want to learn more. The truth is they will only be transformed when they try the practice for themselves. Fruits of centering prayer will be unique to each individual. That makes it exciting.

Improved Productivity

At work I have multiple tasks, and at the end of the day many of them always remain. I constantly review my list and prioritize what needs to get done and what can wait. I have noticed that I no longer panic when I see the size of my list. I calmly work my way through it. I am able to focus on the task at hand and not worry about the other tasks. This is yet another fruit of centering prayer.

At the end of the day, I am always amazed at what I have been able to accomplish. I do still panic at times. However, I notice that I become aware of my anxiety much sooner now. When I notice this anxiety, I let it go. When I let go, I am able to be present—and when I am present, I am able to focus on the task at hand. I let go of other pending tasks and center my awareness on the task before me.

In the evening, I am calmer. I used to have anxiety over all that needed to be done. As a parent and husband, I am faced with a multitude of responsibilities. There is too much to do and not enough time to do it all. But I have learned to let go of this anxiety as well. When I let it go, I can accomplish some of these tasks much quicker. I learned that I do not need to do each task each night. Now, I often wash the dishes in the morning before I go to work. Perhaps I spend more time with one or two of my children and then the next night I spend time with the third one. There are also the nights when I need to completely let go. This means that after dinner I don't try to "accomplish" anything; I simply sit and talk with my wife and kids. Centering prayer has taught me to let go of preconceived notions of how and when household tasks need to be performed.

Excitement for Life

I noticed a new-found excitement for life after months of centering prayer. I love to spend time with my wife. We enjoy watching our favorite

Netflix. We like to go out to breakfast. We relish our time together when we drink a cup of French-press Columbian coffee made to perfection.

I also love to walk in the evening with my daughter. I enjoy our discussions. She talks to me about her writing. She shares with me her drawings. I look forward to when I practice centering prayer with her in the evening. Centering prayer has taught both of us to open to life and what it has to offer.

I also find myself enjoying my younger son more. He often asks me to chase him. We do laps in the family room till we are both exhausted and brimming with laughter. I like to play catch and basketball with him, to pick him up and hug him. He too likes to practice centering prayer with me, and he asks me to do so almost nightly. Most nights we take a one-minute sit together. Centering prayer has taught both of us that we need silence and action. They balance us and make us whole.

I like to listen to my older son tell me what he has learned in school. I am grateful for our talks as I drive him to and from his friends' houses. I like to go out for quick meals with him. I especially enjoy our annual weekend trip to Pittsburgh and our talks during the six-hour drive to and from. We share a love for Pittsburgh Panther football games. We walk and explore the city. This is our special time.

I love to read books and write my weekly meditations. I enjoy when I write guest articles for other blogs. This book has been a great journey. Twice per week, I take scheduled time and write for two to three hours. I love this time and am often surprised by how the words come together on the page.

I love to go to the gym with my best friend, something we have done together for more than twenty-five years. We exercise and have some great conversations about college and professional football and the upcoming weekend.

I teach centering prayer at churches and colleges in the community. I enjoy planning each session and listening to the session attendees share their stories. Ironically, I often learn the most when I teach.

In short, since I started centering prayer, I have an excitement for life that I did not have before. Centering prayer has taught me to let go and enjoy life! I am able to release my grasp on yesterday and tomorrow and be fully present in the moment, to enjoy simple pleasures and the joy of loved ones and community. In all the activities I just mentioned, I am less distracted than before. I am more fully present in the moment.

One of the reasons there are such high numbers of depressed people in affluent and technological societies such as the United States is that people are constantly going in several directions at once. And no one is at home, so to speak. Few are fully present in the moment. They are eating lunch while responding to texts on their phone. They are halfheartedly talking to their child while they stare out the window and muse about problems at work. Centering prayer can counter the trend toward diffuse attention, multitasking, and discontent. It can give us back our centers of gravity and satisfaction.

Discernment

As Amos Smith says in *Healing the Divide*, "In silence there is revelation—revelation about ourselves."[40] In silence, I have learned that I cannot do many things well. However, I can choose to do one thing, and do this one thing well. Silence helps me make wise decisions.

The silence of centering prayer has taught me what is important. At my church, I realized I was overextended. I was co-chair of our membership committee. This meant I greeted new visitors each service, sent a welcome email to them after their visit, held meetings with the others in the committee. And I met with potential new members to answer their questions. At the same time, I was co-chair of the Love Thy Neighbor program. This church-funded program assists those in the community who require rental, utility, and grocery bill assistance. They are generally in between jobs or temporarily suffer from a financial hardship and need short-term assistance. I made certain there was an assigned church member on call each month, which was often me. In short, I organized and administered the program. Last, I led the church's adult education program and conducted a biweekly class before each service.

The silence of centering prayer and a wise wife allowed me to step back and pause. I asked God, "What is it that you want me to do at my church? What skills do you want me to use now? What new skills do you want me to develop?"

God gave me an answer. I decided to focus exclusively on the adult faith education at my church and resign from all my other duties. I also decided to attend church biweekly rather than weekly. If this surprises you, remember, God is not limited to a church building. God's Spirit is active in my home too. My wife has taught me this. She has taught me to trust God—that God always provides, albeit most often not as we expect.

Letting go and giving over the discernment process to God opens us up to new possibilities. It is another form of the letting-go reflex that I have learned in centering prayer. When we release our hold on activities that don't fulfill us, God often nudges us toward activities of substance that do fulfill.

Healing and Transformation

I am a worrier. Each workday I awake anxious about the tasks I need to accomplish at work or at home. I cannot answer why other than that is currently the way I am.

The first thing I do before I start my day is take my twenty-minute centering-prayer sit. It never fails: after each sit I am no longer anxious or worried. I am calm, excited, and ready to start the day. Each day I am amazed by the transformation that has occurred. The healing I need finds me in the silence of centering prayer. God takes my anxieties and replaces them with wisdom and a deep inner peace.

When we sit in silence, we are healed. Silence is a gift from God. God is within the silence and waits to refresh and rejuvenate us. Silence is the place I go to be healed by God. Centering prayer teaches me that I can have inner peace even when there is outer chaos.

An Experience of the Fruit of Centering Prayer

It is 11 at night. I descend into our basement to make certain the lights are off before I retire for the night. As I walk on the carpet, I notice that moisture is squishing beneath my feet.

Then I hear what sounds like a shower. When I investigate further, I find that at the top of the water heater, a spray of water flows. I could literally take a shower beneath it.

My wife has now joined me in the basement. We desperately try to figure out how to turn the water off. We both grasp at multiple valves in the vicinity and turn them all. I finally manage to find the right one. At last, the water is off—but the damage is done. More than half the basement has an inch or more of water on the floor. It's a colossal mess!

My wife calls the insurance company. We decide to go to bed and deal with this mess in the morning. There is nothing more we can do.

In the morning, we call the plumber. The plumber informs us that the water heater burst open, which caused the constant shower spray of water. He advises us to contact a public adjuster.

Within a few hours, at the request of the public adjuster, a team of workers are in our basement. I hear bangs, drilling sounds, and sawing. By the time the crew is done, they have pulled up three quarters of the carpet on the floor and cut out eighteen inches of baseboard from the floor up, also in the same basement area. There are now humidifiers stationed strategically throughout the basement that absorb the moisture. Twenty garbage bags are filled with items that the work crew quickly gathered for our later review to determine potential water damage for insurance purposes. This work needed to be done quickly to stop the potential growth and spread of mold.

While all of this goes on, today is my work-from-home day. I have multiple conference calls throughout the day. Two of my kids have a half-day at school and are both home by noon.

I would not have gotten through this day as calmly as I had if it had not been for centering prayer, which provided a deep inner peace and calm. I did not know where it came from. It surprised me. Centering prayer is indeed a gift from God!

Reset Button

The silence of centering prayer is my "reset button." Silence is God's way to refresh me. All hell may have broken loose in the basement the day before or I may have had a tough day at work yesterday, but today is always new start. I can reset and begin again. The kids might misbehave. I am free to start again. Maybe I am just tired. I did not get enough sleep the previous evening. I can let go and begin again.

I am very busy at work. I cannot seem to catch up. I am behind. I drive to work and the car overheats. I get to work and discover the coolant level is very low. At lunch I drive to Target and buy coolant. I fill the car up and drive home. The next morning I check the level. It is low. I fill it up and drive to work.

The second morning, I check the coolant level. It is low again. Underneath my car is a puddle. Today, I decide not to drive my car and take my wife's car to work so we can take my car to the shop. There was a delay in the repair, and it is now the second day that the car has been in the shop.

My youngest son decides to carry his mini sandbox upstairs. He drops sand all over our steps.

I am shopping with my daughter. She is unhappy because I will not buy her something she wants. Internally, I begin to steam. My car is broken. It is in the shop much longer than anticipated. I have sand all over my stairs. My daughter is upset. I need my "reset button."

My "reset button" is the silence of centering prayer. During centering prayer, I let go of everything. I give my car and my kids to God. I say, "God, you can have my car and my kids. I just want to rest in You for a short while and be refreshed. I want to hit the reset button." I exchange my frustration for the peace of God in Christ. It always seems to work.

Thankfully, every day is not like this. However, it comforts me to know that I have a reset button and that I can begin again. I need this time. I need God to refresh me, to reset me. I need God to recharge, hold, love, and fill me with whatever I need.

Centering prayer not only transforms a trashed day. It can also transform inmates in prison, hurricane survivors who have lost their homes, and teenagers whose hearts have been broken. Centering prayer can transform a myriad messes, dilemmas, and disasters by resetting our frame of reference.

No matter my frustration, grief, or anxiety, after centering prayer I reemerge with an attitude of acceptance, trust, humility. For me, that is the ultimate fruit of centering prayer.

. . . .

Questions for Reflection and Discussion

1. How does it make you feel to sit with God and have no expectations? How is this different from your other forms of prayer?

2. If you have started a centering-prayer practice, what fruits have you experienced?

3. How can you be more present with family and friends during the day? What does this mean? Why is it important?

4. Do you believe centering prayer can improve your productivity at work and at home?

5. How can centering prayer be like a reset button for you?

Chapter 5

. . . .

DIMENSIONS
OF PRAYER

. . . .

Do not worry about anything,
but in everything by prayer and supplication
with thanksgiving let your requests
be made known to God.

—Philippians 4:6

The summit of Christian prayer
is accomplished when you can trust
that you are constantly
in the presence of God.

—Richard Rohr[41]

My life has changed as a result of centering prayer. My approach to God has changed. My relationship with God in Christ has evolved. I have added depth to my prayer life.

Before I began a centering-prayer practice, my prayer life was one dimensional. It was self-centered, selfish. I defined prayer as being when I talk to God, so I brought to God my wishes and desires for the current day and the longer-term future. I brought my wishes and desires for family and friends. Sometimes I yelled at God.

I now think of prayer in four dimensions:

Prayer is when I speak to God.

Prayer is when I listen to God.

Prayer is when I am in community with others.

And prayer is when I rest in God.

Prayer Is When We Speak to God

I believe God does want us to talk to Him. We need to complain to God when we are not happy and vent when frustrated. We can tell God when we are scared, ask for healing when our bodies are not healthy, and seek God's comfort when we are lonely.

It is okay to get angry at God. In fact, it makes perfect sense at times, given the state of our world. Being real with God about our feelings is a sign of intimacy. When it comes to our relationship with God, any and all feelings are acceptable; all were known to Christ. The real killer of intimacy is not volatile emotions but indifference.

We need to bring our concerns to God for family, friends, members of the community and world. God wants to listen to us and wants us to get things off our chest. This is healthy. Repressed thoughts and worries are unhealthy. God loves us! Of course God loves when we feel comfortable enough to approach Him and pour out our hearts like David does in the Psalms. Prayer can also be when I simply let go and say to God, "I do not know." I am okay with that. I just let it be.

Prayer can be as simple as one word. Maybe it is a person's name spoken to God. Sometimes we make prayer more complicated than necessary.

The Jesus Prayer

Amos Smith knew I often prayed the Jesus Prayer, so he sent me a prayer rope. It was hand knotted by Orthodox monks in Greece and shipped from there. Each knot on the rope forms a cross.

The Jesus Prayer, also called the Prayer of the Heart, the Prayer of a Single Thought, or simply The Prayer, is a short, simple prayer. It has been widely used, taught, and discussed throughout the history of Eastern Christianity. The exact words of the prayer have varied, from a simple form, such as "Lord, have mercy," to an extended form: "Lord Jesus Christ, Son of the Living God, have mercy on me, a sinner." I say, "Jesus, Son of God, have mercy on me."

In the Orthodox tradition, the Jesus Prayer is recited with the aid of a prayer rope. It typically has a hundred knots, although prayer ropes vary. Three hundred, two hundred, fifty, and thirty-three knots are all common. There is typically a knotted cross at one end, and a few beads at certain intervals between the knots. The purpose is not to count the knots but to help the pray-er concentrate. The rope's invention is attributed to Pachomius in the fourth century, who was a desert father in Egypt.

I use my prayer rope after centering prayer or whenever I want to. I often carry it in my pocket or leave it in my car. I wear it while I write. While praying, I hold it between my index finger and thumb of my right hand, saying, "Jesus, Son of God, have mercy on _____." In the blank I will say "me" or another person's name or a situation.

After each sentence, I move to the next knot, then repeat the prayer until I no longer have a name or situation in mind.

For me, it is life-giving to combine prayer and action. My fingers' movements help me focus on God. I believe when I say this prayer, Jesus is present and guides me or the other person or situation. (Of course, Jesus is always present. Even when we forget or don't feel like He is, Jesus is always with us.)

At night, I like to walk. Often I spend a good portion of my walk reciting my adapted version of the Jesus Prayer. I don't need to go on and on. I say this short prayer over and over—and let it rest in God. After my centering prayer each morning, I also often recite the Jesus Prayer before I begin the day.

Prayer Is When We Listen to God

A relationship requires more than just verbal communication. If I had a friend who only talked to me and never took the time to listen, I would feel hurt. I too want to be heard. A healthy relationship involves both—speaking and listening. To listen is to open a space for another and let them fill it.

God speaks to us every day. It is we who choose not to notice.

How exactly does one listen to God? Prayer is how we listen to God.

God speaks to me when my six-year-old son interrupts my reading by jumping in my lap, asking, "Daddy, will you chase me?" God speaks to me when I take a walk at night with my daughter and we together look at the night sky lit by the moon and millions of bright stars. God speaks to me when I read a book and amazing insights leap out from the pages. God speaks to me when I listen to a sermon at church, and I hear a perspective I had never heard before. I open a space within to just let it be. There is no judgment. There is no right or wrong. It just is and it is beautiful.

God speaks to me in many ways. I have heard His voice when I arrived early to help prepare for the upcoming church service. A first-time visitor walks through the door. She is obviously distraught and immediately starts to talk. Her husband left her. She needs to take care of her child. She has problems at work. She was driving, saw the church, and stopped on the spur of the moment, looking for a place where she could share her heavy burdens. A group of us listen and reflect back to her what we hear. We ask if she will let us pray for her. She leaves before the service starts, and we never see her again—and yet I am certain that God was speaking to us that morning.

God always speaks. Often, though, we choose not to notice; we choose not to listen.

Prayer Is Community with Others

We are not meant to live in this world alone.

I am an introvert and treasure my time in solitude. I love to read. I wrote this book because I enjoy solitude and placing thoughts on paper. And yet a full life of prayer includes community.

I love to hear my wife tell me about her day. I need to share my day with her as well. She is my witness on life's journey. I enjoy spending time with family. I like to dine with a friend. I love Thanksgiving and Christmas, when the extended families are all seated at the table, ranging in age from six to seventy-five. We talk, listen, laugh, share, hug, and sometimes cry. We are in communion and it is beautiful. It is a form of prayer.

Prayer Is When We Rest in God

Centering prayer teaches me to let go of all thoughts, emotions, and physical sensations. I open and consent to God's presence and action within. I sit quietly. During these times, I do not talk to God. I am in God's presence. I let God act in me.

When I first began to practice centering prayer, I could only last one or two minutes. Then I did it for five minutes and even ten. On June 1, 2014, I decided to sit for twenty minutes, the amount of time that Thomas Keating[42] suggests. I have not looked back.

Centering prayer is a journey into the depths of my heart. It is a journey beyond words, thoughts, images and into the pure presence of God. This quote by Carl J. Arico beautifully describes what happens when we rest in God during centering prayer: "In centering prayer thoughts contain what needs to be healed and the silence creates a space for the healing to take place."[43]

I rest in God during my centering prayer. There are other times when I rest in God—when I walk at night, feeling the wind blow on the back of my neck while I listen to the sounds of the night. When I look at sky, stars, mountains, trees, rivers, lakes, I see the Divine; I rest in the Divine Presence. When I enjoy life, I rest in God. I read a powerful book, watch an exciting movie, enjoy a bike ride on a rural path. These are all times when I rest in God.

Sometimes, I do not realize that I am resting in God. I am afraid to receive a test result from the doctor. I am worried about how my child will perform in school. I am away from home on a trip and miss my wife. God continues to be with me in my worry, fear, and loneliness; it is I who forget. I rest in God even during these times. There is never a time when I do not rest in God. I am just not always aware of it. As my centering-prayer journey unfolds I am more and more aware.

Centering Down

I often do what Quakers call a centering-down practice. It consists of three steps: *release, receive,* and *rest.*

During the *release* step, you place your palms down. This is a symbol of your release to God. You verbally or internally release to God whatever you need to, specific to how you feel at the moment. For example, you might release anger, anxiety, depression, loneliness, or worry. You release these emotions and thoughts to God. You let go of whatever you need to get off your chest. After the release step, you quietly pause for as long as you need to before you move on to step two.

During the *receive* process, you place your palms up as a signal to God that you are open to receive whatever She wants to send. Verbally or internally, you ask God for confidence, compassion, empathy, love, wisdom. The palms-up position is an open posture indicating your willingness to take whatever God thinks you need at this moment.

Step three is *rest*. During this stage, you simply sit with God. You are in God's presence. Feel free to sit in silence for as long as the Spirit moves you.

Centering down can be practiced as frequently as needed. It can also be practiced in community. I once led my church through this prayer during one of our services. At the conclusion, we held a meeting to discuss important church decisions, but first, as a community, we went through each step. We released to God our fears and concerns regarding our church's future. We asked God to bring us wisdom, courage, peace, love, and whatever else we needed to best move forward. Last, the entire congregation sat in silence with God. It was a powerful experience. We united. We became one body. We were, are, and will continue to be the Body of Christ! The Body of Christ in action.

Prayer Is Letting Go

Centering prayer teaches us to live life in an open posture to God. We begin to see God in action around us. We see God in other people, life events, Nature, the sky. Centering prayer opens us to the loveliness of life that God wants to reveal and share. We learn to open our minds and hearts, to see beauty around us that we did not notice before.

Be Open to New Experiences of the Divine

Richard Rohr wrote that, "Prayer is not about changing God, but being willing to let God change us."[44] God is not a genie that grants wishes. I need to rethink how I approach God. I need to let go of my desires, dreams, and wishes—and instead, be open to the desires, dreams, and wishes that God has for me.

In May of 2015, I visited the Won Buddhism Center of Philadelphia. Before I entered the temple area, we removed our shoes. I liked this idea. The first thing I do when I enter my home is take off my shoes. It makes me feel comfortable, relaxes me. Doing this at the Buddhist center, I felt at home.

We began the service with a five-minute chant. I had never chanted for five minutes straight. It seemed like it would be an eternity. Yet before I knew it, we were done.

From the chant, we moved to a twenty-five-minute silent meditation. I knew that this would not be difficult. When I practice centering prayer, I do so with my eyes closed. The silent practice that I was asked to participate in was with my eyes open, looking down the bridge of my nose. Similar to centering prayer, we were told to let go of all thoughts. We were told to ignore any itches. Let them pass. I was pleasantly surprised to discover that I was easily able to meditate with eyes open. The time passed quickly.

We moved from silent meditation to walking meditation, something I had never done. Fifteen of us formed a circle fifteen feet in diameter. We walked slowly in a circle, our pace extremely slow. I estimate the movement from when I placed my left heel down and rolled it until my toes finally touched the ground was three to five seconds before I performed the same action with my right foot. It took some time to adjust to this snail's pace. I needed to focus to maintain balance. Within a few minutes, however, I felt comfortable with the pace and began to enjoy it. Like the sacred word in centering prayer, each step I took during walking meditation was an opening to God. We walked one full circle. I do not know how long it took. It was a wonderful experience. I lost track of time and was at peace.

I entered the spaces between my thoughts. I was in the Presence.

The Buddhist temple experience taught me that contemplative prayer, the pure presence of God, can be found in chanting, silent meditation, and walking. God is everywhere. God waits for us to meet Him in the practice that best suits us. I am certain there are many other forms of contemplative prayer that I can practice, where I will also meet the pure Presence of God.

Quaker Silence

In March of 2014, I experienced a Quaker silent service. The church I attended traced its roots to 1699, though the meeting house where I sat in was built in 1823. The service had no minister. I sat in silence for an hour with one hundred others in a simple room with only benches, windows, and wood floors.

On three occasions, individuals shared a thought. Then back to silence. I heard the rain gently pummel the windows. I heard human sounds: coughing, sniffing, breathing. I heard the wind blow and wood floors creak. I heard my thoughts. Sometimes I had no thoughts, just the spaces between thoughts. The room became a container filled with peace, love, community.

When we are silent we are naked before God. We empty our mind of its thoughts and emotions. We let God's gaze shine directly on us. I do this as part of my daily centering prayer practice but had never done it with a group this large.

At the end of the service, we prayed for each other. We greeted each other and passed the peace. We are meant to experience silence in community with our God. George Fox, the founder of the Quakers, often exclaimed that the most powerful kind of worship is silent worship or what Quakers sometimes call "waiting worship."

Because we live and move and have our being in God, whether we realize it or not, we constantly pray (Acts 17:28). I had heard that life is a prayer, but I did not understand how this could be true. Now I understand that I live in God. I am always connected to God. I cannot disconnect, even if I try. God's presence always remains. Only my own awareness of God's presence comes and goes, depending on the quality of my contemplation.

• •

Questions for Reflection and Discussion

1. How would you define prayer? How do you pray?

2. How has your prayer life evolved?

3. How do you listen to God?

4. What does it mean to rest in God? How have you experienced this?

PART TWO

· · · · · · · · · · · · · · · · · · · ·

Intertwined
with God

To become fully human
is to become fully divine.

—**Thomas Keating**

Chapter 6

. . . .

MY EMERGING UNDERSTANDING OF GOD IN CHRIST

. . . .

God is not a question to be answered,
but a mystery to be experienced.

—Unknown

God is present to everything and to everyone
and is prepared to give Himself to us
if only we are willing to consent.

—Thomas Keating[45]

Our concept of God is formative. It changes as we learn and grow. It forms out of our deepest understandings of who we are in the world and our purpose. Centering prayer has changed how I think about God and Christ.

Early Years

When I was five up until I was a teenager, I believed in and prayed to God. God was in the sky and looked down on me and the rest of us.

For a short while my family went to a Unitarian church. I remember how the children's class bored me. The things I enjoyed were the donuts and drinks after service. We went to this church when I was in elementary school and attended for a year or so. That was my only childhood church experience.

In middle school and high school, I went to a youth group on Thursday nights that was led by pastors at a Baptist church. There must have been fifty to seventy-five teenagers in attendance each Thursday. We sang, performed skits, and listened to a brief sermon. We usually went out afterward to a local diner to hang out. I made a good number of friends. This was my first experience of a Bible-centered church. I accepted Jesus as my personal savior and was told that as a result, I was saved from hell when I died. This group did not believe in dancing. They also wanted to make certain we did not listen to "inappropriate" heavy metal music.

When I invited my dad to a parent night, he was not impressed. He thought they were crazy, though he did not stop me from attending. Meanwhile, I still listened to my music. I still danced. Ironically, the group often hosted roller-skating trips. When you are at a rink, you skate to the melody of music. I call that dancing, but I guess they did not. Nevertheless, I enjoyed this youth group, made many friends, and attended many of their events. I stayed with this group till I was a senior in high school.

As soon as I was "saved,"[46] I began to read the New Testament. I did not understand all I read, but I tried to relate it to how I should conduct myself now. At the time, I did not know that the Bible was a collection of books written by many authors over many hundreds of years for particular communities. I simply thought it was the direct word of God and absolutely inerrant. I thought everything within it was accurate and historically true. I believed I was saved from hell but that others may not be. However, I did not push my beliefs on others.

Post High School

During college I found a youth group and attended their weekly meetings. I also made friends that were not part of the youth group. During my second year of college, I took a break from God. As I look back, I realize I felt guilty for some of my behaviors, so I decided to stop attending the youth group.

After I graduated from the University of Pittsburgh I went back home and got a job. At the time, my parents were members of the United Church of Christ, so I attended church with them. I enjoyed the church and pastor. I made many friends who are still friends twenty five years later. I continued to read the Bible, and I also read many books by evangelistic authors. I read many books by prosperity preachers, and I began to read New-Age books. I explored!

I became very active in my church, was a youth group leader, oversaw our endowment fund, and became vice president. Meanwhile, God was still up in the sky. And I still thought people needed to be "saved" in order to escape hellfire, even though this was not preached at my church.

My Forties

I took a break from church in 2009 and began to explore. I read progressive Christian authors, like John Shelby Spong and Marcus Borg. I began to realize that the Bible contradicted itself. I started to question, Who is this Jesus? Is he both God and human? Was he merely a human? Was he simply a great prophet? If what he preached was not "believe in me and be saved," then what was he here for?

After my three-year break from church, I came across books by Carl McColman—*Answering the Contemplative Call* and *The Big Book of Christian Mysticism*. After reading them, I was hooked. God began to change for me.

God was no longer the Deity up in the sky who looked down at me. God was now as close as my breath. She was within each breath I took. He was even closer than each breath. God was within me, yet also outside of me and everywhere. I began to practice silence.

I discovered centering prayer after reading Amos Smith's book, *Healing the Divide: Recovering Christianity's Mystic Roots*. I began to dabble in it. I read books on centering prayer by Thomas Keating, Cynthia Bourgeault, and David Frenette. I was convinced this was the path for me. The silence of centering prayer connected me to God. Mysteriously and paradoxically, God seemed to be in the silence, outside of the silence, and within.

I was enticed by Cynthia Bourgeault's words: "The promise of contemplative prayer is that if you show up, things will start to change."[47] These words were a nudge into a larger world that unfolded in the years to come.

God Is a Presence

God is Presence. God is always present. It is me who forgets this.

God is in the joy and pain, worry and calm. God is in the anger and inner peace. No matter how I feel, She is in it with me. God's inner peace is always available. It is I who need to open to it. This is where I am right now.

God is Presence. God is in me and with me. I am never apart from Him. That is why centering prayer attracts me. It is my time to sit with this Presence—what the Quaker Thomas R. Kelly called the "real Presence." In other words, this is not wish fulfillment, an exercise of imagination, a human construct, or a fairy tale. I stand with generations of mystics, including Kelly. We are witnesses to the "real Presence" of God.

I don't need to pray. I don't want to pray. Those aren't the words I use anymore. Instead, I want to be held by the Presence. I want to be loved and healed by the Presence. I want to take this Presence with me into my non-centering parts of the day.

Centering Prayer and God

My centering prayer practice has helped me better understand who God is. It has helped me open to God and learn what God wants me to see.

Here is what I hear God say: "I am Presence. Go ahead and sit with Me. Go ahead and ask Me questions. I am always with you. My peace is always with you. I am in everything: people, earth, trees, mountains, waters.[48] I love you. Be present wherever you are. Listen and observe. Use all of your senses. Love others. Do not judge. Sit with Me. Ask Me questions. Wait for the answers."

Spiritual Direction

I now see a spiritual director monthly. I wanted to find someone who practiced centering prayer to glean from her wisdom, to help me go deeper.

After I share with my spiritual director, she says, "And how do you think God feels about that?" The first time she did this, I laughed. I had never thought about that. I figured what God thought was His business, not mine. My director challenged me. For example, I mentioned that during the work week I sometimes wake up anxious and worried about what I need to accomplish. She challenged me to take this to God. She told me to journal my feelings and to speak to God through my writing. After I spoke, she challenged me to reflect on how God might respond to what I shared.

Here's an example of what I wrote.

Me:

On weekdays I awake anxious. I think about what I need to do at work. Sometimes I wake up in the middle of the night. I think of the never-ending tasks that need to get done. I think about the tasks I do not know how to do. I think about the numerous emails I need to catch up on and the new ones that will come. I wonder what new work will come in on top of the work I have yet to complete. This is what makes me anxious. How can you help me, God?

God:

Why do you worry? Why are you anxious? I am with you, Richard. I love you. You are not alone. I am always with you. When you do get anxious, come to Me, and I will give you rest (Matthew 11:28). I love you so much and I do not want you to feel this way. Let's together get these things done. Let's together look at the tasks, prioritize them and one by one get them done. I don't want you to panic.

I am with you and I am in you. My wisdom is within you. My wisdom is at your disposal. Please tap into it. Please never forget this. Together we are powerful. Never forget this. I hope this helps. I don't want you to feel anxious and worried while you sleep and when you awake. I give you My peace. I give you My inner wisdom. I give you My love. My love constantly fills you. Never underestimate the power of My love for you.

I encourage you to try this exercise. Tell God what is on your mind. Speak it or write it down. When you have gotten things off your mind, switch roles. How do you think God will respond to you? Again talk it aloud or write it down. Let the Spirit act in you. Be open to the Spirit's prompts and nudges, love and wisdom. I think you will find this a powerful exercise. Please take the time to both talk to God and then listen. I have continued to take time to do this. God speaks to me through my writing!

I have moved from experiencing God as Someone in the sky looking down upon us to my present understanding of God as Presence. I now experience Divine Presence as accessible at all times, and particularly accessible in silence. This is a huge shift, from distant to intimate, from abstract to experiential.

. . . .

Questions for Reflection and Discussion

1. Who is God for you? How has your experience of God changed over the years?

2. What practices have helped you better connect to God?

3. Do you think a spiritual director can help you on your journey? Why or why not?

4. Do you think posing questions to God and then writing God's response can assist you on your journey? Why or why not?

5. Where do you find God?

Chapter 7

· · · · · · · · · · · · · · · · · · · ·

I AM A
DIVINE BEING

· · · · · · · · · · · · · · · · · · · ·

Do you not know
that you are God's temple
and that God's Spirit dwells in you?

—1 Corinthians 3:16

The image of God
has been woven
into the fabric of our being.

—John Philip Newell[49]

I am on a search to find the true me.

I am a human being. I have a body. My body helps me accomplish many tasks.

I have a mind. I have dreams and goals. My mind helps me plan my actions.

I have thoughts and emotions. They help me express myself to this world.

Am I my body? Am I my mind? Am I my thoughts and emotions? Who am I?

God Is Within Me

I am a human being. I am also a divine being. I am not God but I know God is within me (Luke 17:21). My body is the temple of God (1 Corinthians 3:16). I am a divine being that allows God to express Himself through me. God is within me; God is within all of us. We are made in God's image (Genesis 1:27). Some of us know this. Some of us do not. Some ignore it. Some deny it. Jim Marion reminds us, "All we need to do to be saved is to consciously realize who we have been all along. We need to realize our divinity, own it, take up the responsibility of it, and live it."[50]

When I slow myself down, I remember I am a divine being. This is what happens during centering prayer—my sit with Jesus.

My "sacred word" is an interior image of Jesus that is based on an ancient icon.[51] As my thoughts wander or my emotions reflect the past day or upcoming events, I ever so gently return to this interior icon to bring me back to my purpose for centering. I consent to the presence and action of God within. I expect Jesus to show up.

The first three stages of prayer are:

1. We speak, God listens
2. God speaks, we listen
3. No one speaks, both listen.

I allow myself to enter the fourth stage of prayer that Irwin J. Boudreaux describes[52]—no one speaks, no one listens. I rest in God.[53] I let God act in me. What will God do? I do not know. I do not need to worry about it. My job is to rest and to trust. God's actions within will be later revealed in my various actions during the day.

Throughout the day, I ever so gently return to my sacred icon when I find my thoughts and emotions distract me from what I need to do. I recenter myself during my non-centering portions of the day. When I become anxious, angry, or frustrated, I mentally visualize my sacred icon and bring myself back to the task at hand.

During centering prayer, I consent to the Divine, so the big "D" and me, the little "d," sit with each other (Divine and divine). We become united. During my non-centering parts of the day, I do the same. My little "d" recognizes that I need to become one with the big "D." I mentally visualize my sacred icon and allow myself to become united with God. This allows me to get back to the task at hand and partner with God to accomplish the tasks that lie ahead.

Since I began my centering prayer practice I have noticed a few new things about myself. I am much calmer. Yes, I still become anxious, nervous, frustrated, and upset, just like everyone else. Yet I notice that I am able to calm myself much more quickly and resume whatever tasks are in front of me. I no longer panic when I have an enormous list of tasks that need to get done in a short period of time. I know the calmness and fluidity of this process is because of centering prayer! God and I partner throughout the day.

Centering prayer slows me down, and I bring this slowness into my daily life. I am calm yet more productive. I am tranquil and make wiser decisions—and as a result, I am able to get more done. Paradoxically, I find that to work faster does not mean I will get more done. When I work slowly with a calm intensity, I am more productive.

To Love Is to Listen

The sun shines. The Pleiades illumine. Pacific Ocean waters roar. Sycamore branches extend into the sky. Bright white and yellow daisies bloom. Jaguars roam, hunt, and eat. These non-human creations are in a state of *being*. They are free to fully express what the Creator wants them to be! God is within all that exists, from the Milky Way galaxy to the tiniest atom in a squirrel's tail.

And God is within me. I can decide to respond to this Love that is within me; I can choose to let it flow out of me and into the world in inspired words and deeds. I can also choose to see this Love in others. I can accept this Love from others even as they accept the same Love that flows from me.

How can I let this Love in me flow into the world? One way is to listen to people. We are all in such a hurry to speak. When we listen, we often do not really listen. We only think about what we plan to say. We love others best, however, when we just listen. We give people the space to show up and speak their truth. When they speak their truth, we are on holy ground.

Some of my most joyful moments are when I quietly sit with my family. All I do is listen and watch. We enjoy each other's presence. At mealtime, for example, I ask questions and then quiet myself to listen. My son shares funny stories from his day at middle school. My daughter discusses her drawing class at the community college.

I enjoy listening while I volunteer at Manna on Main Street soup kitchen in Lansdale, Pennsylvania. Manna provides a hot meal for those who would otherwise not have one. When I volunteer, I greet the people who enter. They often come in with big smiles and hilarious comments. They joke with me when I forget to bring back all the food they requested. I tell them to give me a break; this is not my full-time job. We chat. I offer them a beverage and ask them what they want to eat. After I bring them their meal, I ask if they are still hungry and seconds are always offered. But the most important thing I do is listen. It is a time for me to be quiet. This is all they want. They want to know someone cares about them and will hear them. I may never see them again, but that doesn't matter. What matters most is that I listened to them. They leave with a smile and raised spirits, as do I.

There are so many people in our world who feel sidelined or discarded. So, when we give people the time of day, instead of whisk them along, it can have a profound effect, beyond what we imagine. There are stories of people who decided against suicide based on someone taking time to listen. Deep listening that leads to understanding is the greatest gift we can give to another person.

Perfect Love Casts Out Fear (1 John 4:18)

God is love (1 John 4:8). God is within me. When I forget this, I live in fear and worry. I am afraid to take on new tasks and afraid to experience unfamiliar things. I lack confidence.

When I forget that God is love and God is within me, I often make the wrong choices. Or I make no choice. I freeze. I stop movement forward. I procrastinate. I complain. I blame others. I'm unhappy. As soon as I remember that God is within me, though, I no longer have any reason to fear. I am free—free to explore. I am free to experience life, free to love and be loved.

James Finley wrote that anxiety comes from our estrangement from the consciousness of God's love inside of us.[54] Once we remember who we are and Who is within us, we have no reason to fear.

Solitude and Community

I enjoy my time in solitude when I read a book, practice centering prayer, take a walk, drive, and sit alone in a coffee shop. I need this time to refresh, release pent-up emotions, laugh, and on occasion cry. I need this time to connect to God, to reconnect to the Divine.

I also crave community. I need time with family—to sit at the dinner table, talking and laughing; go to the park to slide and dangle from parallel bars. As a family we spontaneously jump in the car and get ice cream or go to the arcade.

I work from home a few times per month. My wife works full time from home, so this means we get to have a cup of coffee together, eat breakfast together, and enjoy conversation.

I love to watch college football—especially with my sister! My sister and I are not in the same room—she lives four hundred miles away—but we text each other during the entire game. I also watch football with my nephew. We cheer and we boo. We eat. We talk. We catch up on each other's lives. I need this time to yell and scream. I need this time to be with another person. It makes me whole.

My time in solitude enriches these times with others. When I am more deeply present to myself, I am more capable of listening and truly being in the moment with others. They go hand in hand. When I have known deep relaxation and Presence in centering prayer, I am more capable of relaxing and letting my guard down with my friends and family.

Christ Lives Through Me (Galatians 2:20)

I can accomplish great things. They are not great because of the attainment of fame, riches, or prestige. They are great because I let God act within me.

These words from *Jesus Manifesto* by Leonard Sweet and Frank Viola spoke directly to me: "He doesn't want us to imitate Him: instead, Christ, the Unspeakable Gift, wants to live in and through us."[55] I know if I live my life with this in mind I will accomplish many great things (Philippians 4:13). More important, these things will be great because they line up with God's will for me.

During centering prayer, I "consent to God's presence and action within."[56] During my non-centering prayer times, I let God's presence and action within me motivate my external actions. I then let the Spirit's action within me during centering prayer motivate my actions in all areas of my life.

I also allow God to act within me when I practice verbal prayer. During my verbal prayer, I ask God questions and wait. I continue to ask God the same questions throughout the day. I might ask God the same questions day after day until I think I have an answer. I want God's action to motivate my external actions, and so I will come to God in both centering prayer and verbal prayer.

Who I am and how I think is often hidden from others until I have the courage to speak and act. I am not me when I do what others want me to do. I am not me when I do what I think I should do. I am only me when I act in accordance with what my inner divinity nudges me to do. My inner divine nudges are the actions of God within. How do I discern that these nudges are from God? When these nudges are accompanied by feelings of inner peace, freedom, spaciousness, excitement, joy, gratitude, and clarity . . . then I know that their origin is God. These feelings are indicators of God's presence and action within. If these actions will benefit others, I know they are God's will.

If I am nervous to try something new, it does not mean I should not do it. It means I have forgotten that God is within me.

God Refreshes Me.

When I took my first breath, God breathed into me. Each time I inhale, God continues to breathe into me. I know this because the mystery of God is present everywhere. As I inhale, God's Spirit refreshes my soul.[57]

I am reminded of this by the verses of Psalm 23: "The Lord is my shepherd, I shall not want. He makes me lie down in green pastures; he leads me beside still waters; he restores my soul." The New International Version says, "He refreshes my soul," which means make like new, give new life, rejuvenate, replenish, breathe new life into. Each time I inhale, God refreshes my soul. She restores me to the person I was created to be. I have a God whom I can come to freely, Mystery who delights in the refreshment of my soul.

I do this as part of my centering prayer practice: I let God refresh my soul. When I awake and take my first silent sit before I begin the day, God refreshes my soul. As the day's tasks weigh on me, my reservoir empties. I take a second sit and once again let God refresh my soul. God refills my reservoir and we partner to continue the day.

Before . . . After . . . Forever

"If you came out of somewhere then you had to be somewhere before you came."[58] I have a "before." Until I read this sentence by John O'Donohue, I never thought about my "before."

Who I am is not my body. I know that because, as I understand it, my body's cells die and are replaced by new cells numerous times over my life.

Before my birth experience, I came from God, and I will return to God. I continue to evolve in my understanding of my connection to my Source. I evolve as I remain open to Spirit's presence and my connection to others. I do not need a body to be connected to God, since God does not have a body.[59] God is Presence. God's Presence is all pervasive and continuously creates.

Before my body existed, I was in God. During my bodily birth, God released me into this world, but He still wants me to remain connected, with the hope of future intimacy and union. Death will be a continued connection to God.

Rather than worry about where I came from, I focus on where I go. I connect with God and others. I let God take me where I need to be. I open my mind. I enter nondual awareness of the bonding agent that holds all things together, including the cells in my body and the spiraling galaxies. I open my mind to all experiences and withhold judgments.

I came from Great Mystery. I live connected to Luminous Presence. I die into Magnificent Unity. I rest assured that whether I live or die,

suffer or celebrate, "All will be well and all manner of things will be well."[60]

Be Still and Know That
I Am God (Psalm 46:10)

I have spoken this verse to myself for years. Its
meaning continues to evolve for me. When I first
began to recite this verse, I did not know what
to make of it. I thought to myself, "Of course You
are God. So what! What does this mean? What
are You trying to tell me?"

Then it became, "Just sit and rest in God's
presence." It stayed this way for a few years. I
just didn't know what to do with it. I knew there
was more . . . so I waited. After a few years, this
verse changed to mean, "Know that I am a Divine
being." God is within me. Divine Mystery is not
just out there but is within me.

Most recently, this verse has evolved to mean
just *know*. Know what? "Know that God is always
with me." God nudges me to move and take action.
God wants me to move past fear, take risks, do new
things. She wants me to stretch my comfort zone.
He wants me to move past the safe distance and
trepidation, and to reach out a hand to help. God
wants me to take the risk and show up and be who
I am. "Know" means God will walk side by side

with me as I try something for the first time. God is within me, partnering with me to push all limits wherever they might be within my personal life, family life, faith journey, and career. I look forward to how this simple verse will continue to evolve. I will continue to speak it to myself. I will continue to listen and then go where God takes me.

The End of Fear (1 John 4:18)

Jesus not only said that He was the light of the world but that we too are the light of the world (Matthew 5:14). Jesus tells me I am a divine being. God is within me (Luke 7:21, 1 Corinthians 3:16).

I know there is nothing in this world that I need to fear. Wherever I go, God is with me. When I don't know how I will complete the multiple tasks at work on time, I know God will be there. When I nervously await test results at the doctor, I know God will be with me. When a close friend or relative passes away and I grieve, I know God will be with me. When I am afraid to try something new, God will be with me.

Because I am a divine being, when I move forward I know all will be okay. This knowing gives me confidence and freedom. It gives me life. A letter written to John Spong speaks strongly to what this knowing means to me: "to answer God's call to live fully, love wastefully, and be all that I can be."[61] I am free to do this because I am a divine being.

The Journey Within

I am a beginner. Each day I get up and I put on the "Mind of Christ." I remind myself that I am a divine being with a little "d." I am work in progress. I am a beginner each day and that is okay!

Centering prayer is my daily practice that helps me put on the Mind of Christ. I let go—and freefall into the Mind of Christ. When I have the Mind of Christ, I, like Jesus, recognize that I am intertwined with God. "I am in God and God is in me" (John 14:20, 14:11). This is nondual thinking.

I have learned to let things be. I have learned to let go of judgment and be more open to life as it is. My eyes are open to see the beauty all around me without the need to make critical evaluations.

I do not understand God (Isaiah 55:8). Tony Jones writes, "The East emphasized that theological insight was gained from mystical experiences with God; the West preferred academic study and intellectual debate."[62] I, like the Eastern experience of Christianity, now believe that God is beyond academic study and intellectual debate. The more we study God, the more we put our human definitions and limitations on God. We create God in our own image. We create a God who justifies our actions. We create a God who satisfies our needs. We create a God who makes us happy. Yet God is not a construct we can manipulate. God is a Mystery that pummels us from within and without, transforming us into who She intends us to be. I best understand and study God when I let go and let God teach me. The only way to do this is to relinquish control. I let God take the reins.

Tony Jones also writes that "the Orthodox . . . firmly believe that God lives inside of us. We reach God when we journey within. Jesus came to reignite that spark of divinity within us."[63] Centering prayer is part of the journey into this spark of divinity within. We will best learn who God is when we let God teach us. How will God teach us? When we connect with Jesus during silent prayer, we will connect to our inner divinity. We will let God in us act through our outer actions. We allow God to guide us, both internally and externally.

Our human bodies are animated by the actions of the divine spark within—what the Contemplative Outreach Community and Thomas Keating refer to as "the divine indwelling." We cannot separate human and divine. We are not all human. We are not all divine. We are both. They act together. Centering prayer brings the two together for beautiful action.

If we only live as humans, we can do some terrible things. If we think, "I am God," we act from our intoxicated ego. If we join the two through silent prayer, however, we get action that is divinely correct—God-inspired actions. I pray that Christ ignites this spark of the divine within so I can use my human body to give birth to responsible, compassionate, and loving actions. I pray the same for you.

• • • • • • • • • • • • • • • • • • • •

Questions for Reflection and Discussion

1. Do you believe we are divine beings? Do you believe your body is the temple of God? Why or why not?

2. How do you connect to the divine within?

3. Does your time in solitude enrich your time in community? Why or why not?

4. What are some practices or activities that you can do to allow God to refresh your soul?

5. What does Psalm 46:10 mean to you? *Be still and know that I am God.*

6. Jesus tells us we do not need to fear. Do you believe this? Why or why not?

Chapter 8

. . . .

WHO IS MY TRUE SELF?

. . . .

Depression is the result of
being separated
from one's true self.

—**Alice Miller**[64]

I cannot imagine a sadder way to die
than with the sense that
I never showed up here on earth
as my God-given self.

—**Parker Palmer**[65]

When I am depressed, I often wonder why I feel this way. I know God loves me. I know God has placed unique gifts and talents within me. I also know that God expects me to take action (but God will not *force* me to take action).

I know that I am never absent from God. Yet, I often freeze. I take no action. It is as if I would prefer to be depressed. Sometimes I am just plain scared to act.

Meeting people is difficult for me. I am anxious about approaching people I don't know. I do not know why I feel this way. I just know that is the way it is. Sometimes I feel very alone. Often, I will isolate myself so I do not need to meet new people because doing so scares me. The truth is, however, I *do* want to meet new people.

I am also afraid to try new things. I will often avoid unfamiliar activities. I don't know why I do this other than I just do. Again, however, the truth is I *do* want to try new things. I want my life to be exciting. I want to be free of this anxiety. I want to feel joy.

I watch my six-year-old son when he plays. He laughs spontaneously. He is not self-conscious about life. He just does it. He is free and alive. I want to feel joy like he does. I want to have my son's freedom, to feel this same inner peace. If I can feel this same freedom, perhaps I will no longer have anxiety when I meet new people. If I have this same freedom, perhaps I will more easily try new things and feel the joy that is associated with fresh experiences.

I want to be happy, relax, laugh, let loose, express myself. I want to be confident and feel secure. I want to express my humanity. All of these expressions are contained within my true self. They just need to be freed.

Who is my true self? My true self is calm, content, and unafraid. It is filled with life. It experiences God's love. But to become my true self is very difficult and requires ongoing struggle. According to Richard Rohr, we have to fall into our true self.[66]

I need to fall out of my "self" into my true self. When I die to self, I awake to my true vocation. I become the self God intended me to be. The core of my true self is a deep knowing that I am beloved and cherished by God. That who I am and the choices I make matter to God.

Silence Connects Us to Our True Self

I sit in silence to reconnect with my true self. Silence teaches me who I am. I am not the competing interior voices that scream for my attention.

I am loved by God. Sometimes during centering prayer, I feel God's exquisite love for me, which makes all the difference. It is not hypothetical or spoken. It is experienced, not only in my mind, but in my physiology and nervous system. It wafts over me.

Centering prayer helps me reconnect. It helps me remember who I truly am. I am loved by God. God loves me just the way I am. I no longer need to feel anxious. That is not who I am. That is not who God sees. God sees Her child with unique gifts and abilities that She has planted within me. God waits for me to let them loose in the world for Her and others to see.

My true self is the divine spark of Love within. It is filled with my unique gifts, humor, and personality. It is who I am. Richard Rohr says my true self is indestructible.[67] It cannot be embarrassed. It cannot be offended. When my soul and body act in unison to let the light of Christ shine, I have freed my true self.

Paul Coelho wrote, "There comes a time when our personal calling is so deeply buried in our soul as to be invisible. But it's still there."[68] My true self hides buried within.

I know God is love. Then, what is not love? It will be different for each person. It might be fear, anxiety or self-pity. It might be envy, greed, or jealously. It might be blame, excuses, or grudges. It is anything that often rests comfortably between God and my true self. Whatever it is, it must be let go. All these reactions and emotions are layers that come between God and my true self. They do not allow the two to interact, much less commune. They do not allow the two to unite as part of their natural expression. Let them go! When I do, my true self and God will intermingle. We intertwine and create a path that I can call my own. We soar (Isaiah 40:31).

The Search for My True Self

Who is your true self? I suppose some of us know who this is. Most of us still search. Others do not even think about it.

My true self is the God within who waits to be expressed. He is best expressed when I push aside the small me. The small me is in the forefront when I feel angry, jealous, insecure, afraid. The small me is expressed when I do not listen or accept someone whom I view as different from myself.

My true self is calm, confident, content, unafraid. It quietly listens with no judgment. My true self accepts love and speaks love. It is embodied when I remind myself that I am connected to the Divine. My true self is more than connected to the Divine; it is united with the Divine. My true self is absorbed in Divine love and that is all that really matters. Brennan Manning says, "Define yourself as one beloved by God. This is the true self. Every other identity is illusion."[69]

Every day my true self yearns for expression. Thomas Merton wrote, "But in all that happens, my one desire and my one joy should be to know: 'Here is the thing that God has willed for me.'"[70] When I know the thing that God has willed for me, I am ready to let my true self act. Each day, I must discover and know this thing. More important, I must take action. I need to actively express my true self. The true self must be expressed as visible action in the world. When we encourage the true self by giving it expression, it expands. When we suppress the true self, it contracts.

What a joy it is when we have clarity about what God has put us on the earth to do! Everything seems right with the world. Some kind of interior alignment happens. A calm comes over us; we exclaim, "Yes, this is it!"

Every day, I need to remind myself of who I am in the eyes of God. How God sees me is what matters most. I am a one-of-a-kind individual. God made me the way I am. God loves me as I am. God has a unique purpose for me to fulfill.

I need to accept who I am—and ask God to reveal to me who I am. God has planted many seeds within me. Together we will water these seeds and watch them grow.

When I compare myself with others, that will not show me who I am. When I compete with others, that will not show me who I am. When I choose to not take on a new challenge because I am afraid, that stops me from being who I am.

My job each day is to be who I am.

How Centering Prayer Shapes Who I Am

During centering prayer, I empty myself of my false self. My false self can be many different things, depending on the day. I might be lonely or worried, angry or frustrated. I might be tired or insecure. None of these are who I am. When I let go of them, I am at peace. I discover that I can now get on with my day and the tasks ahead. The distractions and preoccupations end and my real work begins.

I have a proclivity for centering prayer and understand how it can help me and others. I do not want to keep centering prayer for myself. I want to share it. I want centering prayer to change others' lives as it has changed mine. I want to plant centering-prayer seeds so others can see how the gift of silence can be a life changer.

I write articles about centering prayer and place them on my website and share them on other sites. Links to these articles are tweeted and posted on my Facebook page. I tweet one-sentence quotes that share my thoughts and fruits experienced as a result of centering prayer. I teach an adult faith class at my church. Every once in a while at this class, I will teach a lesson about contemplative prayer. During church services, I have shared contemplative prayer practices and led the congregation through centering prayer exercises.

When I see a friend in duress, I briefly share how centering prayer has changed my life and suggest that they try an abbreviated version. I reach out to churches in my community and ask if they would like me to teach centering prayer. Many have accepted my offer. Last, I have written this book, which I hope will open the eyes of others to this beautiful path.

I have gravitated to areas of service in my church that require presence and listening. I am part of our caring ministry. When members are ill, I reach out to them. This will involve an email, phone call, or visit. . They don't want to hear me; they simply want to be listened to. They want to know someone cares. They are in crisis. They are worried. Mostly, they just need to talk. They might be lonely or bored. My simple presence can be a comfort. This time is about me being there in a caring and loving way. My presence and attentiveness makes them feel important, needed, and valued. To hone my listening and presence skills, I will continue to practice centering prayer. The two work together well!

Centering prayer leads me into a place where I can let go. I am one with God. God prays in me. God speaks to me with a "still small voice" (1 Kings 19:12).[71] God wants me to let go of all that I am not so I can be who I am. I will continue to practice centering prayer so I can continue to let go of who I am not and be who I am. I want to be my true self every day. To be my true self is my vocation. It is who I yearn to be.

The Breath of God

Kabir wrote, "He is the breath inside the breath."[72] God is life—the Life within Who waits to be expressed.

God patiently waits to be expressed in both my inner and outer world. How do I allow God to be expressed? I recognize God's breath within me. I rest in God. I set aside my ego. How will I know I do this? I will know it when I see the fruits of the Spirit in both my inner and outer world: love, joy, peace, forbearance, kindness, goodness, faithfulness, gentleness, self-control will flourish (Galatians 5:22–23).

To set aside my ego and rest in God is a daily battle. Daily, I let go of nervous energy and distractions and pray to God that I may rest in Her loving arms. Daily I ask God to help me sense Her breath within me. This will free God to express Herself in both my inner and outer world. Breathe God. *Breathe.* From this center I can move mountains (Matthew 17:20).

The Pretense of Separateness

I am not alone. We are all connected. All of us are connected to God. God is at the center. We are all spokes connected to the Divine hub. When all spokes are connected, the wheel turns. Beauty and miracles are created. When we forget this, the wheel does not turn.

We are never alone. We have God. We have each other. We are not meant to live lives of solitude. We are meant to be in communion with others, family, friends, church members, co-workers, neighbors. When we each do our part, the parts placed together make the whole. If the parts are not placed together in community, there is no wholeness. There is no creation.

I have taken many hours of solitude to write this book. However, I do not write this book alone. I share my chapters with Amos Smith, who edits, questions me, and challenges me to make my statements and thoughts concise. Amos sometimes adds brief comments to clarify. My wife and family give me the freedom to take the time to write. My wife reads and provides her input. I am at the gym and I bounce my thoughts and ideas off of my friend. He encourages me and pushes me. He reminds me that if I help just one person that is all that really matters. Much of what I write is what I have experienced in community with others. This book would never have been published without my community.

John Philip Newell reminds us:

> Prayer or meditative practice is about being dis-membered in order to be re-membered. It is about descending into the death of the ego in order to be reborn from our true depths. It is about being stripped down to our essence, where we will find the gold of our being, the greening power of the soul.[73]

I do this as part of my centering-prayer practice. I let go of all thoughts and emotions, goals and ambitions. I let go of my worries, concerns, and pride. I even let go of God—of who I think God is. I forget me. I dis-member me. I am in the spaces between my thoughts. I am naked in the presence of God (Genesis 2:25).

When my centering prayer session ends, I re-member me. I am reborn. I act from my true self. I need to dis-member and re-member daily so I can continue to act from my true self. Even during my non-silent parts of the day, I let go. I dis-member and re-member. This is a life-long process of renewal.

Our True Self Remains

Our true self is who we are. Nothing can take it away.

My father passed away from Alzheimer's. Despite suffering the symptoms of this terrible disease, my father's true self survived. Through the layers of disease, his true self remained intact and untouched by Alzheimer's. His humor, love of music and food, and listening skills shined through to the end.

I remember listening to a recent *On Being* episode, where Krista Tippett interviewed a psychologist who has led support groups for early-Alzheimer's patients.[74] The psychologist discussed an Alzheimer's patient who looked at his spouse and said, "I don't know who you are but I know I love you." His true self was still intact. His true self was full of love. It was full of love that he poured out upon his lifelong spouse.

Our true self is free. What is our true self free from? It is free from our need to control and manipulate. When we connect to our true self, we are truly free—free to live life and enjoy it. We are free to celebrate the present moment, to give to life and to receive from life.

Our true self has been given to us by God. It is our most unique, authentic, and vibrant self. It is our essence that will shine through outer layers of disease, old age, and death.

Fear

Brian Zahnd stated, "I observe there really are only two forces that move people: Fear and Love."[75]

Fear is a barrier to our true self. It stops me from acting in love. Fear prevents me from talking to someone I view as different. Love asks what I can learn from someone different today. Fear says I do not like change. Love explores, always seeking new things to experience. Fear is afraid to act when an injustice is incurred. Love aids another human being when harmed.

Fear forgets that God is present. Love knows God is never absent. Fear divides; love unites. Fear paralyzes growth; love transforms. Fear hoards; love shares. Fear is temporary; love is eternal. We live, move, and have our being in God (Acts 17:28)—and this God is Love (1 John 4:8). Love connects us to our true self (1 Corinthians 13).

Let Your True Self Shine

Jesus took Peter, James, and his brother John and led them up a high mountain by themselves. There, He was transfigured before their eyes. His face became as dazzling as the sun, His clothes as radiant as light (Matthew 17:1–3). During centering prayer, I may not physically shine, but as I reconnect with my true self, which is hidden in Christ, I let it shine.

George Fox, the founder of the Quakers, often referred to the "light of Christ" within. This is our radiant source with profound potential that awakens through prolonged exposure to stillness and silence in centering prayer.

During centering prayer I ever so gently let go of all the barriers and obstacles that are between God and me. I sit naked before God (Genesis 2:25). I let all of God's Presence sit with me and shine directly upon me. I let God do whatever

God wants to do within me. I let God work in me without analysis or evaluation.

Perhaps this means God will fill me with love, healing, wisdom, confidence, insight, or mental or physical strength. Or perhaps God will simply fill me with more "contemplative eyes." By this I mean the ability to be more open, to not be so quick to judge right versus wrong, to let things be. To hear an opinion different from mine and consider new things. To simply say "yes" to life and all it offers.

Centering prayer can also put us in touch with challenging emotions that we have yet to fully process. If this is the case, we sit with the emotions and let them run their course. It is completely up to God. In centering prayer, we surrender to whatever God reveals in the present moment, before any labels of "good" and "bad" are applied by our reasoning faculties.

When I get up from centering prayer, I get on with my day. I continue to do my best to gently let go and continue to connect with the presence of God that is all around me. I also do my best to continue to let my true self shine, reflecting, in some small portion, Jesus' light that shone from the mountain. The "uncreated light" or "eternal light," as referred to by the Eastern Church, is manifest in different orders of magnitude from the stadium floodlights of the saints to flickering candles of the weakest soul—and yet it is the light of Christ that permeates all.

Awakening Our True Self

Centering prayer awakens our innermost point of being—our true self, which wants to love and create.

Phileena Heuretz teaches that "contemplative prayer practice is a commitment to loving our self so we can love others well."[76] I sit in silence to love God and to let God love me. I sit in silence because I love myself. If I cannot love myself, I will not be able to love others. If I cannot accept the love of God, I will not be able to love others. When I say I love myself, I do not mean, however, that I am full of myself. I mean that I am a precious child of God. I love because God first loved me (1 John 4:19).

One aspect of love is comfort level. We are comfortable around people we love. And people who lack a wholehearted love of self are not completely comfortable in their own skin. As we become more deeply familiar with ourselves through prayer, we put people around us at ease. As we become more intimate with God's languages of silence and stillness, we become more comfortable with Divinity, and all that this word signifies.

When our own divinity naturally emerges, we become more creative and loving. This is not because of any effort on our part, but because of God's quiet work within.

• •

Questions for Reflection and Discussion

1. Who is your true self?

2. When do you most feel your true self?

3. Who is your false self?

4. How do you know when you act from your false self?

5. How is fear a barrier to your true self?

6. How can you continue to let your true self shine? What practices can help you to let your true self shine?

PART THREE

. . . .

Jesus'
Humanity

Jesus had to become like his
brothers and sisters in every respect.

—Hebrews 2:17

Chapter 9

. . . .

HISTORICAL
JESUS–
AN OVERVIEW

. . . .

Jesus is what God looks like in sandals.

—John Dominic Crossan[77]

Exploring the various perspectives on Jesus is of the utmost importance for Christians, because He is our window into God. He is God in sandals.

Other world religions have defined their unique testaments—their unique angles on God or ultimate Reality. Jesus is Christianity's angle.

If you want to see God, look no further—look to Jesus (John 14:9). Distilled Christianity is the knowledge and love of Jesus. And an important aspect of the knowledge and love of Jesus is an understanding of the Jesus of history.

Where was Jesus born? Who were His parents? What can I glean from His life events? What can I learn about the Judaism He practiced? What was the corner of His world like when He grew up? How did the Roman Empire impact Him? Why was He crucified? Was He resurrected?

This will not be an exhaustive scholarly study that answers those questions, but I will share what I have learned. My sources are books I read and lectures I listened to from the following scholars and historians: John Dominic Crossan, Marcus Borg, N.T. Wright, and Luke Timothy Johnson.

To discover the Jesus the Gospels tell us about, N. T. Wright declares, we need to get inside them. This means I will let the four Gospels tell me about Jesus. Before we start, I need to be clear, that the Jesus of history is a vital part of the Christ of my faith. It's not possible to separate them. The historical Jesus was a real man who lived on this earth—and He was God.

"To journey with Jesus means listening to his teaching—sometimes understanding it, sometimes not quite getting it."[78] These words from

Marcus Borg's *Meeting Jesus Again for the First Time* echo my experience. Sometimes I get Jesus. Sometimes I don't understand what He meant. I have learned to trust. I meet the Jesus of my faith in my centering prayer, and I believe that my practice will open my eyes. And I meet the Jesus of history and communal faith in the pages of the Gospel. There is continuity between the two! Jesus' presence in prayer and His words preserved for centuries open my eyes.

The Jesus of history spoke in aphorisms, parables, and stories, which impact me today and inform my faith. Generally speaking, these parables are not linear and nondual. Jesus was also known to regularly venture to lonely places and pray (Luke 5:16). His example shapes my prayer life.

The Beginning

Jesus was born around 4 BCE in northern Palestine. He grew up in Nazareth, a small village about one hundred miles north of Jerusalem that consisted of a few hundred brick and mud homes. Nazareth was a very small, insignificant village. The population was probably anywhere from two hundred to two thousand people. The village had no school and no roads.

Jesus' mother, Mary, was related to priestly families. His father, Joseph, was from the ancient royal family, the family of King David, of the tribe of Judah. Joseph was in the building trade, which placed their family in the second lowest rung in society. Jesus' family did not own land; they were poor.

Jesus probably had four brothers and an unknown number of sisters. We know very little of his early life. Bible scholars speculate that Joseph died before Jesus began his public ministry.

Jesus Was Jewish

Jesus' parents were Jewish, and Jesus remained a Jew His entire life. He did not create Christianity; rather, He reformed Judaism.

From an early age, Jesus was taught to read Israel's ancient scriptures, the Hebrew Bible. He knew them well. Luke's Gospel tells us that at twelve years of age, He was in the temple, asking key theological questions and debating with the adults (Luke 2:41–52).

Within the diversity of Judaism were shared core convictions: radical monotheism, promise, and hope. Radical monotheism meant God is one. God alone is Lord and is to be loved with all the heart, strength, soul, and mind (Deuteronomy 6:4-5). The promise and hope was that God had entered a covenant with Abraham and Sarah. He had promised they would have many descendants who would live in their own land.

Jesus may have gone to school in the synagogue in Nazareth, where the emphasis would have been on reading and writing the Torah. (The Torah is the first five books of the Hebrew scriptures.) As an adult, Jesus spoke as a Jew to other Jews. His followers were Jewish. All the authors of the New Testament were Jewish, except possibly the author of Luke and Acts.

Woodworker

Jesus worked with His father in the family business, the carpentry trade. This means Jesus probably made wood products: doors, door frames, roof beams, furniture, cabinets, boxes, yokes, and plows. It is possible that as a teenager into his late twenties, Jesus helped rebuild the city of Sepphoris.

Sepphoris was a city north of Nazareth, about an hour's walk, which was the largest city in Galilee, with a population of forty thousand. In 4 BCE, after the death of King Herod the Great, Judas the Galilean, son of a local bandit named

Ezekias, attacked Sepphoris, sacked its treasury and weapons, and armed his followers in a revolt against Herodian rule. As a result of this insurrection, the Roman Governor in Syria, Verus, as reported by Josephus,[79] burnt the city down and sold its inhabitants into slavery.

Herod's son, Antipas, was made governor and rebuilt this city to include palatial mansions, Roman theaters, aqueducts, paved streets, markets, residential houses, public buildings, bathhouses, and synagogues. This was a wealthy city, a major Jewish town and the center of the Jewish administration in the Holy Land, as well as the commercial center for the whole area. Wealthy, cosmopolitan Jews lived there, as well as Romans, Greeks, and Arabs. It is not specifically mentioned in the Gospels, but most likely Jesus visited this city, probably frequently, and He might have worked as a carpenter to help with the rebuilding effort. This would help explain Jesus' wisdom, which often reflects a larger world view than that of a rural tradesman.

The Banks of the Jordan

We know nothing of Jesus' adulthood until He shows up on the banks of the Jordan to be baptized by John the Baptist (Mark 1:9). At this point, Jesus abandoned His life as a carpenter, left Galilee, and crossed the Judean desert to where John and his disciples were preaching. We don't know why Jesus did this. We simply know that something led Him at around the age of thirty to leave behind His life as a carpenter.

John the Baptist may have been an Essene, although his ministry differed from theirs in several ways. Like John, the Essenes withdrew from society and practiced a simple life, but unlike John, they were a closed community that did not evangelize the way that John did. One well-known Essene monastery was Qumran, which was within walking distance of the Jordan River, where Jesus was baptized by John. Despite their differences, John may have visited this community and received support from it, emotionally and spiritually. If this is true, then it is possible that Jesus also visited Qumran, and may have even lived there for a time. This would explain some of Jesus' monastic leanings, especially the glaring absence of Jesus' wife, which would have been virtually unheard of for a Jewish man his age.[80]

John believed he had a message from God. The great cleanup was to come. You better repent (Matthew 3:2).

After John the Baptist was arrested and executed, Jesus took a different angle (Matthew

14). Jesus had inherited John's ministry, but He believed that God's work was all about collaboration. The Kingdom was to be entered. It was a process. It will not happen if you wait passively for God to take action while you do nothing. Jesus' message was about collaboration and participation in God's Kingdom as it unfolds in the here and now.

The Kingdom of God

What is the Kingdom of God? The Kingdom of God exists when the poor will be fed, the naked clothed, nation will no longer war against nation, and people's hearts will be centered on God. The Kingdom of God is both a personal and a social transformation. We are called to transform our relationship with God, others, and ourselves. We are also called to resist and combat social injustice in the world. We are the eyes, ears, hands, and legs of God. Social transformation is the fruit of inner transformation! The question we each need to ask ourselves is, "How will I participate in God's Kingdom?"

During Jesus' time, the Jewish people had been under foreign occupation and oppression for centuries by the Assyrians, Babylonians, Medo-Persians, Greeks, and now the Romans. The Roman emperors proclaimed themselves as gods. The Jews were divided in their response to the Roman dominion. The Zealots' call was to rise up and rebel. Meanwhile, the Herodians and Sadducees felt that to resist the Romans was futile; they decided to make the best of the situation and cooperate with the Roman rulers. The Essenes created an alternative society in the desert. The Pharisees believed the Lord would deliver everyone as long as one became purer and more righteous like them, not like sinners such as prostitutes, drunkards, tax collectors, and Roman collaborators.

Now into the mix comes Jesus, who announces a new message: "Repent," which means change your way of thinking. Believe the good news. The Kingdom of God is now available to all.

"If you want to be my disciple," Jesus taught, "you must hate everyone else by comparison, your father and mother, wife and children, brothers and sisters and yes, even your own life" (Luke 14:26). The poor in spirit, those who mourn, the meek, the pure in heart, the peace makers, the persecuted— all these will be blessed, said Jesus. If your hand or your foot makes you sin, cut it off and throw it away. It is better for you to lose part of your body but have life forever. Love your enemies and pray for those who persecute you (Matthew 5).

What are we to make of this? What did Jesus mean? These are some key themes. Jesus calls us

to love God, love others, and yes even love ourselves. We are called to practice radical inclusion.
All are loved by God and welcome in this kingdom,
and we too are to love all. There are no more labels:
no more male/female, Jew/Gentile, slave/free, rich/
poor (Galatians 3:28). We are challenged to resist
and combat social injustice. Distributive justice is
the order of the day! All are entitled to food, shelter,
clothing! We are called to help others that need our
assistance whether we assist individually, through
our church, or through larger organizations that
have the scale to alleviate social injustices.

Last, Jesus challenged us to search our hearts
and deeply reflect upon our inner thoughts. Our
thoughts, Jesus taught, are just as bad as our
harmful outer actions. Hateful thoughts are just
as destructive as when we physically hurt someone. Lustful thoughts are as bad as unfaithful-
ness to our spouse (Matthew 5:27–30, 23.23-28).

The Kingdom of God is what the world would
look like if God sat on Caesar's throne. This
Kingdom has two aspects, present and future. It
is available in this present moment; that is the
proclamation of mystics. It is also to come (future
tense) when the hungry have enough to eat, the
naked are clothed, and the sick are shown compassion; that is the proclamation of prophets. The
kingdom of God is distributive justice not retribu-

tive justice. God owns the world, and everyone is entitled to get a fair share of it. The kingdom of God is also within. It is when we lead God-centered lives as opposed to self-centered lives.

In *The Dawn of Christianity*, Robert J. Hutchinson writes, "In recent years, even many secular New Testament scholars have rejected the idea that Jesus was an end–times prophet proclaiming the imminent apocalypse." Robert goes on to say, "So what was Jesus' vision of the kingdom of God? According to the records we have, when Jesus spoke about the kingdom, he said it was 'good news' (Luke 4:43), 'like treasure hidden in a field' (Matthew 13:44), not bad news. He compared it to a wedding feast, not a cosmic artillery barrage (Matthew 22:2-14)."[81]

The kingdom of God was the action of Jesus. He healed people physically and mentally; He forgave prostitutes, tax collectors, and everyone else, including those who society considered unworthy. He gave the so-called unworthy a seat at the table and ate with them (Mark 2:16). He even partied and celebrated with them (Luke 7:34). He accepted and loved them (John 13:34)! He made them feel whole. He healed them to their innermost core. This is what the Kingdom of God looked like: it was healings, celebration, forgiveness, and a renewed heart.

For God's Kingdom to come in a collective sense is for those on the margins of society to be treated with respect and dignity, and to be given justice. When the Kingdom comes to a society, no one is discarded or cast out. All have God-given worth. For God's Kingdom to come in a personal sense is for us to feel that all those things that we hide, suppress, and deny about ourselves are welcomed by God. No aspect of our personality or history is shunned. Everything has its place. God can even use the most difficult aspects of our biographies and personalities as catalysts for transformation. If God can even transform a wicked symbol of oppression and torture, like the cross, God can transform any and all things.[82]

Why did Jesus do all of this? N. T. Wright proclaims, "No point putting the world right if the people are still broken."[83] The Jewish people waited for the kingdom of God. They waited for YHWH Himself to come and rule as Israel's King, removing this world's corruption and oppression. They waited for God to bring justice and equity. Jesus' ministry is what it looks like when God is King. This is what Jesus was doing!

Parables, Sermon on the Mount

After John the Baptist's death, Jesus went back to Galilee and spent most of His time in the small countryside towns around there. It was a short ministry that lasted three years before Jesus headed to Jerusalem. What happened in this short period?

Jesus spoke in parables. He made people think. He did not explain the parables, but instead He pulled people in and engaged them. He made them question their preconceived ideas and think in a different way. Jesus challenged people: "Are you with Rome or with God?"

The Sermon on the Mount is the real Jesus— His real teachings. This was His social vision. I share these teachings in chapter 9. Jesus' movement was inclusive and multiethnic. I like this point that Richard Rohr makes: "Jesus consistently ignored or even denied exclusionary, punitive, and triumphalistic texts in his own Jewish Bible in favor of passages that emphasized inclusion, mercy, and honesty" (Luke 4:19).[84] His movement was one of radical inclusivity and hospitality. Love always came first.

Nonviolent Resistance

Jesus was a nonviolent resistor (Matthew 5: 38–40, 44, 26:52). He was not passive but His methods were not violent. He became the exemplar for many nonviolent leaders to come, such as Leo Tolstoy, Gandhi, and Martin Luther King Jr.

Jesus' words had political ramifications. The Romans reasoned that if they executed Jesus, this would put a stop to this nonsense, and so He was executed for acting like He was the king of the Jews. The Romans viewed this as a credible threat. If Jesus was a violent resistor, the Romans would have executed not only Jesus but His whole band of violent resistors. This is what the Romans did. They would have wiped out the whole lot of them. As we know, they did not. They only executed Jesus.

The Jews did not execute Jesus. As a whole, they did not reject Him. A small but powerful elite group of Jews, whose power was derived from the Romans, turned Jesus over to the Romans. He was a threat to them and to their power. As we know, however, the execution of Jesus did not stop His movement. It continued to grow and expand.

The Four Strokes of Jesus

I like what Marcus Borg refers to as the four strokes of Jesus: spirit person, teacher of wisdom, social prophet, and movement founder.[85]

As a *spirit person*, Jesus had an experiential awareness of the reality of God. Jesus prayed and fasted. He often went off on his own and prayed for hours at a time (Luke 5:16). Most likely Jesus practiced a form of contemplative prayer, which would have been common among John the Baptist and the Essenes. Matthew 6:6 is most often interpreted as "closing the door" to the senses (practicing contemplative prayer).

Jesus addressed God as Abba, His Father. This was an intimate and personal relationship that was not a common tradition at this time. For Jesus, God was not just an outside Source. God was in Jesus and Jesus was in God. The Spirit of God emanated from Jesus. Jesus lived His life connected to God—God nourished His soul. He spoke with authority that flowed from His spiritual experience. As a spirit person, He taught the need to die to the conventional wisdom of the world and to die to the self. Jesus wanted the Spirit to transform lives. Jesus wanted people to be centered in God.

As a *wisdom teacher,* Jesus taught in parables and memorable short sayings (aphorisms). He was both a teacher of wisdom and the embodiment or incarnation of Divine wisdom. His parables and aphorisms invited His hearers to see something they might not otherwise see. He wanted to open eyes to a new perspective. He invited people in and made them think for themselves. He did not give them the answers. He wanted people to find the answers for themselves.

As a *social prophet,* Jesus criticized the economic, political, and religious elite with His alternate social vision. He was often in conflict with the authorities. The dominant social vision was centered in holiness and purity codes. Jesus stressed that compassionate acts, not purity codes, were central to God's vision (John 15:12). God was not concerned with purity rituals that were important to the Jewish temple priests and officials. Instead, God was concerned that compassion be enacted in the community (Luke 6:1–11). Everyone was welcome at the table. For Jesus, purity had to do with internal motivations, not outward observances.

Lastly, Jesus was a *movement founder.* He reformed Judaism. His was an inclusive movement that included women, the poor, the sick, the tax collectors, prostitutes, and marginalized. It also included people of social stature who found His vision attractive.

Jesus went to Jerusalem to make His final appeal to the people at the center of their national and religious life. There, He was sentenced to death by Pilate on the charge of treason and executed by the Romans as a political rebel. Jesus did not create Christianity. After His death and resurrection, His early followers gave birth to Christianity.

Healer, Intelligent and Courageous

Jesus was highly intelligent and had remarkable verbal gifts. He was clever in debate. He answered questions with yet better questions and left His challengers speechless. Many of the day's theologians tried to trap Jesus in His words, but He would outmaneuver them (Matthew 22:15–22). As Marcus Borg states, "In contemporary terms, he was both a right-brain and a left-brain thinker."[86]

He ate meals with the marginalized (Matthew 9:10–11). He entered Jerusalem on a donkey and mocked the Roman leadership (Matthew 21:1–11). He overturned tables in the Temple (Matthew 21:12). Jesus courageously made strong social and political statements. His friend John the Baptist was executed, yet Jesus continued His work, even though He had to know His life too was in danger.

Jesus healed. The Bible is filled with stories of the healings He performed and the people who left their previous lives to join Him (Mark 1:34–36). Jesus attracted crowds (Mark 5:24). There was something about Him that drew people to Him. Despite the briefness of His life, His impact was powerful.

Jesus, the Son of God, and God's Kingdom

Jesus was a spirit person who had an intimate relationship with God. He was a social prophet and a movement founder. He invited His followers to participate in the same intimate relationship He had with God. Jesus invited His followers to form a community whose social vision was shaped by the core value of compassion. He invited us to see what God was like. Jesus invited us to journey on the path with Him.

The Jewish people believed that the Temple was where God lived. They saw Heaven as God's space and the Earth as human space. The Temple was the one place where both overlapped. N. T. Wright tells us, "Jesus was behaving as if he were the Temple, in person."[87] This is critical. Jesus is God in person. We no longer need to go to the Temple to be with God. God is with us. God is with us in the person of Jesus.

Jesus never explicitly explained the concept of the Kingdom of God. Is the Kingdom of God a final kingdom brought by the Jesus, the Human

One? Is it to mean the end of the world as we know it—or is it when we participate in and collaborate with God to change the world? Theologians don't agree.

Concluding Comments

Marcus Borg makes some interesting points about Jesus: "He was a remarkably free person. Free from fear and anxious preoccupation, he was free to see clearly and to love. His freedom was grounded in the Spirit, from which flowed the other central qualities of his life: courage, insight, joy, and above all compassion."[88]

I believe Jesus was free because he and the Father were One. God was His Abba. He grew to know who He was and what it was that He was supposed to do. He took time to pray and be in silence. These times prepared Him for the action He was to take. For me, Jesus embodies both the messiness of our humanity and the blessedness of the Divine. Throughout the Gospels, a creative tension always exists between these two aspects. That's what makes the Gospels so dynamic and compelling.

Marcus Borg reflects, "Though the story of the historical Jesus ends with his death on a Friday in A.D. 30, the story of Jesus does not end there."[89]

Here we are some two thousand years later. The story is far from over. The historical Jesus has died, but the resurrected Jesus, the Jesus of our faith, is very much alive and a powerful force in this world. He is a life-giving force in my life. I sit with this force during my centering-prayer practice. I arise from each sit resurrected with new life.

Jesus is an exemplar for us of what the Kingdom of God looks like. It looks like Jesus. When God is central and becomes King in our lives, we begin to mirror the life of Jesus—a life that was simultaneously messy and blessed.

. . . .

Questions for
Reflection and Discussion

1. What if anything surprised you about the life of Jesus in this chapter?

2. What do you believe was the Kingdom of God that Jesus announced?

3. Do you agree with Marcus Borg's four strokes of Jesus: spirit person, wisdom teacher, social prophet, movement founder? Why or why not?

4. Why do you think some two thousand years later we still are speaking about this man Jesus?

Chapter 10

· · · · · · · · · · · · · · · · · · · ·

JESUS' TRANSFORMED HUMANITY

· · · · · · · · · · · · · · · · · · · ·

In Jesus we have found
that God is extraordinarily interested
in what it means to be human.

—**Tony Jones**[90]

The Incarnation reminds us
that the spiritual journey is a human one.
Jesus had to deal with His humanity
and He set an example for us.

—**Carl J. Arico**[91]

I want to embrace my humanity. I want to be robustly human like Jesus was human.

My humanity includes those aspects that I hide, suppress, and deny, but are still loved by God. What aspects do I hide, suppress, and deny? I will come clean with one here. Perhaps you too share this aspect.

At times, I am not confident. I should speak up more during staff meetings at work. I know I have more to say at church meetings. Even among friends, I don't always share what I think. When I want to share my thoughts, ideas, and suggestions, I clam up. No words come out. Afterward, I am disappointed with myself. Why didn't I speak up?

I guess I do this because I am afraid that what I say will not be relevant. It will not make sense. It will not add any value to the discussion. Will anyone care? Will what I say even compare to the other more intelligent, well-spoken, and articulate comments made by the others? I am not in their league. Wow! Yes, sometimes these thoughts are in my mind. Are they in your mind too?

What can I do about them? I need to take a step back. Who am I? I am a child of God. I am deeply loved by God. God is within me and waits to be expressed. God has planted something special in me. If God is in me, I need to share this Spirit. God's voice within me is important. It needs to be heard in the world. I often forget this. When I forget this, I lack confidence.

Jesus' Holistic Embrace

Something about Jesus energizes ordinary folks—the Galilean fisherman, and you and me. Jesus hasn't accepted the bill of goods sold in our market economy, that the top wage earners and consumers matter most. Jesus sees beyond the shallow scripting of our society to the deep, most often hidden, Divine imprint on our souls.

I need to remember who I am. I am a child of God. The seed of God is within me and waits patiently to be expressed in this world. It needs to be expressed. Of course, as I do this, I also need to respect others as they express the seed of God that is planted within them.

Surprisingly, when I express my true self, my gifts meet the world's needs. I am fulfilled. My purpose is fulfilled. And I simultaneously impact the world for good. There are things I know and have to say that will bless the world. There are other thoughts that are not yet ripe and should be shelved until they are ready to be shared.

One more very human aspect that I hide and deny—sometimes I am lonely. I am an introvert, so this does not help. I will not be the one in the room who begins and ends the discussion. If I am in a setting where I do not know anyone, it is difficult for me to introduce myself. I become insecure and then I become lonely. It becomes a vicious cycle. Have you ever experienced this? When this happens, I know what to do. I remind myself who I am. I am a child of God. Jesus holds me in His embrace.

Jesus' Robust Emotional Life

Jesus expressed a full range of emotions and sensations: hunger (Matthew 4:2), thirst (John 19:28), fatigue (John 4:6), sadness (Luke 19:41), anger (Mark 3:5), joy (Luke 10:21), and wonder (Matthew 8:10). He was compassionate (Matthew 9:36) and loving (Mark 10:21). At times, Jesus was calm in the face of storms, including when He faced His own arrest. He experienced an agonizing death on the cross, and He felt the agony of separation from His Father (Matthew 27:34–54). If I had to come up with a single word for Jesus, it would be "wholehearted." He did not hold back. He had a contagious zeal.

Why is it important to acknowledge the full range of Jesus' emotions? Because they reveal God in human form—God who comes to earth to experience and share life with us, to show us a new and a better way to live. Jesus embraced His humanity, and we too are called to embrace our full humanity, which includes a full range of emotions and vigor. Jesus said "I have come so that you might have life, and have it more abundantly" (John 10:10).

Jesus' Forgiveness

Jesus modeled forgiveness. When Peter denied Him three times prior to the crucifixion, for instance, Jesus forgave him.

The resurrected Jesus was with the disciples in Galilee, sitting around a fire and eating breakfast. The last time Peter saw Jesus, he had denied Him. Can you imagine the guilt Peter felt? Jesus leans in and asks Peter this question: "Peter, do you love Me?" Three times Jesus asks Peter, and three times Peter answers that he does love Jesus (John 21: 15–17)

Throughout this exchange, Jesus instructs Peter to "feed My lambs, tend My sheep, feed My sheep, and follow Me." If Peter was concerned about being forgiven, Jesus had moved on. He had forgiven Peter, and now He had other things on His mind. Jesus then prepared Peter for the important work that he was called to do. Peter would go on to deliver a significant open-air sermon during Pentecost (Acts 2). Later, Paul affirmed that Peter had the special charge of apostle to the Jews, just as Paul was apostle to the Gentiles (Romans 11:13).

In the Gospel of John, Jesus also forgave a woman taken in adultery. The teachers of the law and religious law keepers brought a woman who had been caught in the sexual act. They exclaimed to Jesus that Moses said in the Law that a woman like this should be stoned to death. They wanted to know what He would do about it. Jesus paused, doodled on the ground with His finger, then calmly said, "Anyone of you who is without sin can throw the first stone at her" (John 8:7). One by one, they each went away until Jesus was left alone with the woman. Jesus asked her if any man had said she were guilty. She told Jesus that no one had, and He replied that He too did not say she was guilty. "Go your way," He said to her, "and do not sin anymore" (John 8:11).

Jesus demonstrated forgiveness all the way to the last moments of His life. As He hung on the cross at Calvary, He exclaimed, "Father, forgive them, for they don't know what they're doing" (Luke 23:34). Jesus said this despite the Roman soldiers that cast lots for His clothing (Matthew 27:35), the same Roman soldiers who had mocked

Him, spit on Him, beat Him, whipped Him, placed a crown of thorns on His head, and nailed Him to the cross (Matthew 27:29, John 19:18). Jesus said this even as the crowd taunted Him and He was all alone.

The life of Jesus reveals the power of forgiveness. He was betrayed—and He loved the person who betrayed Him. One of His closest friends denied Him—and He loved His friend anyway. He was forsaken—and He kept on loving those who had forsaken Him. He was tortured—and He forgave His torturers. He was murdered—and He even loved His murderers. His life shows us Divine forgiveness.

Can I forgive others as Jesus did? I do not know, yet I know I must try. It is obviously a core part of God's human expression.

Jesus' Nonviolence

Brian McLaren wrote, "Jesus has taught that the nonviolent will inherit the Earth. Violence cannot defeat violence. Hate cannot defeat hate. Fear cannot defeat fear. Domination cannot defeat domination."[92]

This is often contrary to how we want to act. It is certainly not how we see nations both past and present act. If someone says something spiteful to us, often our first reaction is to strike back. We want to make a strong statement. We will not be stepped on. We will not allow anyone to walk all over us.

When we drive on the highway and a car cuts us off, we get angry. We blast the horn. We make a gesture. We yell. Or perhaps we're sitting at a traffic light, waiting to make a left turn. The light turns green, but the car in front of us refuses to move. Again, our initial reaction is to blast the horn and curse. Even if no one hears our words, this is still hateful behavior. It is not the loving behavior that reflects Jesus.

Let's look at one more common example. We're standing in line at the store. The person ahead of us asks the clerk many questions. He seems oblivious that I and others stand waiting behind him. Some of us begin to huff and puff internally and even externally. We cough; maybe that will get his attention. Perhaps we decide to say something and later feel guilty about it. Or perhaps we don't feel guilty about what we said.

These are simple situations that happen to all of us. How will we act? What choices will we make? Will we choose the way of love— or aggression?

These trivial situations may seem insignificant, yet sometimes seemingly insignificant gestures and words can set someone off on a good or bad tilt for the rest of the day. People's emotional states often are cumulative, depending on what has happened that day. A kind word can have a more profound impact than we imagine—and likewise, a harsh, angry word can also be powerful in a negative way.

Jesus' Emphasis on Community

Jesus believed that the community must take care of its members (Act 2:44–45).

I was reminded of community and what it means at my son's high school graduation ceremony. As I drove him to the ceremony, we had a nice discussion in the car. He admitted that he was both nervous and excited. "I did it!" he said to me.

"Yes you did!" I replied. "And I am so proud of you!" I reminded him that he will never be alone. "Mom and I will always be there for you."

Later, I sat in the school gym on folding chairs with my wife, our youngest son in my lap. We were joined by my mother, my wife's sister, and my son's cousin. Thoughts raced in my head. *My youngest son is in my lap, while my oldest son graduates. Where did the time go?*

The music began, and the graduation class walked in. My eyes began to tear. Awards were presented. Three students gave speeches, sharing their journeys. The students reminded the audience that their journeys were possible because they were never alone. They had the support of many people: parents, siblings, friends, teachers, counselors. They each thanked their support system. They each shed tears as they reflected upon the loving support they had received.

Jesus teaches us the same lesson that was so evident at my son's graduation: we are connected to others. We do not live alone. When one of us falls—and we will—someone always seems to be there to hold us and lift us back up. We are a community that takes care of its members. A community loves its members, but it also invites strangers in and exclaims, "We love you. You are welcome here!"

Adam Bucko and Rory McEntee wrote: "We need the support, the encouragement, the trust, the love of a community to become fully human."[93] Community is where our humanity can safely express itself. Community is where our humanity flourishes. It is where we come to be supported, encouraged, and loved. It is vital! Jesus knew this. Everyone was welcome at His table.

The power of community was so significant to Jesus that He said, "Where two or three are gathered in My name, I will be with you" (Matthew

18:20). In other words, Jesus and the Holy Spirit are available and responsive to us in community.

The Freedom of Jesus

When I was ten years old, the neighborhood kids gathered as it got dark. There were twenty of us, and we split into two teams. The boundaries were seven houses, front and back yards.

My team was "it," and we stood on the base and counted to a hundred. Our job was to find and tag the other team. If we successfully tagged a member of the other team, they needed to stand by the base (which was usually a tree). When we captured all members of the other team, it was our turn to hide. There was one catch. If someone from the other team was able to run to the base, tag it without capture while he yelled, "Freedom!" the captives were free to escape.

This is my parable for the life of Jesus. The lies we are told about our self-worth entrap us. The lies we are told about hyper-individualism lock us up. Lies about stuffing and suppressing our emotions limit our freedom. Lies about the sweetness of revenge and that violence is redemptive trap our hearts. And then Jesus frees us with His holistic embrace, forgiveness, nonviolence, and emphasis on community. He yells, "Freedom!"

Sermon on the Mount

The eight Beatitudes within the Sermon on the Mount are beautiful descriptions of how to be fully human. Brian Zahnd's *Beauty Will Save the World* describes each one.[94]

Blessed are the poor in spirit, for theirs is the kingdom of heaven.

—Matthew 5:3.

Those who are poor in spirit will be welcome in the Kingdom. Jesus says to all of you who are not very good at being spiritual that today is your lucky day. The Kingdom of God is also for you. It is for everyone, not for a select few. Jesus will meet you where you are in your spirituality. He will fill any holes with His grace if you humbly allow Him in. This is what I do during centering prayer. I let go. I humble myself and let Jesus in.

Blessed are those who mourn, for they will be comforted.

—Matthew 5:4

Sorrow is a part of human life. When we allow ourselves to grieve, we create the space to allow another to comfort us. We need to share our sorrow in community. Sorrow is not meant to be repressed. It needs to be shared. When we share our sorrow, we also learn to have compassion. We need to weep with those who weep. Speaking our truth, getting real about our emotions is cathartic; it releases pressure; it shatters the illusion of isolation and separation. It levels the playing field. Together we can bear each other's burdens.

Blessed are the meek, for they will inherit the earth.

—Matthew 5:5

We do not need to be aggressive, bold, and self-assertive to get what we want in this world. There is another way. The better way is a way of trust and relaxation. God will provide our portion. She will provide our security. We do not need to obtain our lot in life by force and domination. Violence and aggression are not the means.

When Jesus rode into Jerusalem at Passover on a donkey, it was a deliberate act. He was rejecting the militaristic means of empire. He was making a declaration that the meek are not weak! The meek have tremendous strength. Their greatest strength is their faith.

Bold, aggressive, and self-assertive people are often not genuinely secure and confident. They think they need to act in this manner to make up for some lack. This is the only way to obtain what they need. Jesus shows us that there is another way. Jesus shows us that meekness has its own kind of power.

Blessed are those who hunger for righteousness, for they shall be satisfied.

—Matthew 5:6

The fourth beatitude is a political one. Jesus introduced a new way to structure society, one that cares about social justice. He envisioned a world where all people are provided with food, clothing, and shelter. This is a world where all people are paid adequate wages and receive proper medical care. Jesus challenges us to take care of each other. We need to open our eyes to gang violence, predatory lending, sex trafficking, climate change, disdain for the poor, political despotism—and expose it all. We must take action when we see social injustice. Any action is better than doing nothing.

Blessed are the merciful, for they will receive mercy.
—Matthew 5:7

Synonyms for mercy include: compassion, sympathy, understanding, consideration, concern. This is a cruel world that thirsts for mercy. Mercy should be our default setting. People should come to us for mercy. They should come to our churches and find mercy. If people cannot find mercy in our churches, our churches need to change.

The fourth and fifth beatitudes work together. A passion for justice must be tempered by a commitment to mercy. Mercy must triumph over judgment. People were attracted to Jesus because in Him, even the worst "sinners" found mercy. The people labeled "sinners" in Jesus' time were the very poor, prostitutes, tax collectors, and lepers. According to most of the religious types of Jesus' time, these people had been condemned to their condition by God and deserved what they got. But Jesus accepted all these people, which was an outrage to the elite who had a clear definition of "clean" and "unclean," definitions that Jesus spurned. He made the marginalized feel whole. He healed them to their innermost core, teaching them that they were not condemned but loved.

Blessed are the pure in heart, for they will see God.
—Matthew 5:8

One of the ironies of the Gospels is that the sinful and irreligious were often quicker to recognize that Jesus was sent by God than the devout and religious. The religious were not able to see God because of their spiritual pride. They felt justified in judging others because of their moral superiority. For these people, it was very difficult if not impossible to see God at work in the lives of others of lower social standing.

When we acknowledge our own sins and flaws, we are slow to judge others. When we withhold judgment, we begin to see God at work in the world and in the lives of others. A pure and open heart is open to God. A pure and open heart sees God! This is what a contemplative practice such as centering prayer helps us to do. Unlike human love, there are no limits to the love of God.

The Message translation of Matthew 5:8, says, "You're blessed when you get your inside world— your mind and heart—put right. Then you can see God in the outside world." If I am motivated by compassion, my inside world is right. If I act on compassion, my outside world is right.

So many spiritual teachers, including the Dali Lama and Karen Armstrong, proclaim that compassion is the core of the world's religions.[95] And as the different cultures and ideologies of the world continue to collide in the twenty-first century, compassion will save the day. It will literally mean the difference between the cooperation and survival of our species—or our disintegration and ultimate extinction.

Blessed are the peacemakers, for they will be called children of God.
—**Matthew 5:9**

Before Jesus was crucified, He said, "Peace I leave with you; my peace I give to you. I do not give to you as the world gives. Do not let your hearts be troubled, and do not let them be afraid" (John 14:27). The Romans kept "peace" through violence. If you were viewed as an enemy, the Romans conquered you. Jesus brought peace by forgiveness. The only way to eliminate your enemy was to love them. Forgive them. Reconcile with them. Become friends. This is the path to peace! One of Abraham Lincoln's famous lines was, "Do I not destroy my enemies when I make them my friends?"[96]

Blessed are those who are persecuted for righteousness' sake, for theirs is the kingdom of heaven.
—**Matthew 5:10**

Jesus understood that those who practice the Kingdom of Heaven's principles as stated in the Beatitudes will be persecuted by the current powers and authorities that run society. Doing the right thing is often hard and fraught with resistance. We practice the Beatitudes despite the persecution we will face. Jesus states that it is then that we will be blessed and received into the Kingdom of Heaven. We are to persevere despite the persecution. If the church has any longstanding legacy, it is persistence and perseverance in the midst of persecution and suffering.

The Beatitudes beautifully illustrate how we are to live within the Kingdom of Heaven. This kingdom is not a future state. It is here and now.

The Beatitudes do present a challenge. They are often at odds with the many elements of our society: governing establishments, schools and universities, corporate workplaces, and even our churches.[97] We must decide which principles will govern our lives—those of the prevailing powers and authorities or those of the Kingdom of Heaven.

When God sets up His Kingdom, He will do it through the people He calls, equips, and enables. If God will bless the world, it will be through people who take the Beatitudes to heart and live them.

. . . .

Questions for Reflection and Discussion

1. Jesus expressed a full range of emotions and sensations in the Gospels: hunger, thirst, fatigue, sorrow, anger, compassion. What does this tell you about Jesus?

2. Jesus modelled forgiveness in the Gospels. Do you think you can model forgiveness? If so, how?

3. Do you agree with the author's rendering of the Sermon on the Mount? Why or why not?

4. Do you believe Jesus embraced His humanity? Why or why not?

PART FOUR

. . . .

The Jesus Paradox

For in Christ the whole
fullness of deity dwells bodily.

—Colossians 2:9

Chapter 11

· ·

JESUS AND NONDUALITY

· ·

Whatever you did for one of the least of these
brothers and sisters of mine,
you did for me.

—Matthew 25:40

I am convinced that Jesus was the first
nondual religious teacher of the West,
and one reason we have failed to understand
so much of his teaching, much less follow it,
is because we tried to understand
it with dualistic minds.

—Richard Rohr[98]

What is nondual thinking? Many people have not heard of this term or if they have, they don't understand what it means. I continue to struggle and be challenged by the concept.

Richard Rohr explains dualistic thinking like this:

> The dualistic mind is essentially binary, either/or thinking. It knows by comparison, opposition, and differentiation. It uses descriptive words like good/evil, pretty/ugly, smart/stupid, not realizing there may be a hundred degrees between the two ends of each spectrum.[99]

Rohr also comments that dualism "is the ego's preferred way of seeing reality. It is the ordinary 'hardware' of almost all Western people, even those who think of themselves as Christians."[100] Nondualism, on the other hand, transcends differences and dichotomies. It brings unity rather than division.

Nondual Living

Because my normal everyday thinking is not nondual, my actions are also not nondual. I have to struggle to maintain a nondual posture because the world we live in is dualistic. It is competitive, a world where I must succeed. I must show what I can do, what I can accomplish. I must outperform my co-worker if I want that new position. I must outperform my co-worker if I want a better raise or bonus. We live in a world where it seems that the mantra is "compete."

Anger is an outcome of dualistic thinking. Someone does something different from how I prefer to do it, and that makes me angry and uncomfortable. I have to remind myself that maybe there are other ways to think and do things. Why does there have to be a right and wrong way to think about things or do things? Right and wrong, either/or, win or lose—binary thinking is hard to get away from. It is heavily scripted into us from childhood, especially in the West.

Is there another way? Why can't there be enough for everyone? Why can't everyone win? There is actually no need to compare, compete, divide, judge, split the field. All that gets so tiring! We need to move beyond this way of thinking and doing things. We need to say "yes" to everything! Obviously I don't mean we say yes to injustice, hatred, or cruelty. I simply mean that we say yes to reality as it presents itself to us in the moment, without immediately determining if it is good or bad. Some things that seem bad at the outset turn out to be good and vice versa. I am talking about a receptive posture, as opposed to a closed one.

Richard Rohr reminds us that "We in the West are naturally educated in dualistic thinking, so much that we call it 'thinking.'"[101] This dualistic thinking barrier is limited! We need a new lens of both-and, of holding creative tension between opposites, of humor, of paradox, of striving for win-win agreements, instead of win-lose. A nondual view is panoramic, a dualistic view truncated. Our dualistic thinking and seeing causes us to miss the beauty the Creator has provided.

Nonduality and the Kingdom of God

In his book *Putting on the Mind of Christ,* Jim Marion claimed that Jesus is a master of nondual consciousness. Marion also wrote that "the single most important thing that Jesus taught about the Kingdom of Heaven was that 'The Kingdom of God is within'" (Luke 17:21).[102]

If we want to find the "Kingdom of God," it is an inner journey. In other words, the transformation into holistic vision and nondual thinking is subjective, not objective. Objectivity implies an observer and an observed phenomenon, which is inherently dualistic. Nondual thinking, on the other hand, affirms the mystics and the field of quantum physics—that observer and observed are intricately connected. Likewise, we cannot have buyers without sellers; the one implies the other. They are part of one single dynamic called "the sale." We cannot have life without death or Easter without the Crucifixion. They are part of one cycle of life, one gospel narrative.

Jim Marion went on to say, "The Kingdom of Heaven that Jesus saw so well is a vision of this world that sees no separation (duality) between God and humans."[103] We are all in this thing called life together, yet we act like we are not. We do not realize that we are in God and God is in us—and we are all in each other. One could even say that we are like different cells in the same body. If these cells war against each other, it is ultimately self-destructive. The cells will only war against each other because they don't see the bigger picture of the one body, because of the illusion of separation. Of course cells are different, have different functions, and some are more sophisticated than others, yet the point remains: they ultimately form a larger unity (1 Corinthians 12:12–27).

As I look out into the world I see that we do not act as one. I must earn money to maintain my standard of living and take care of my family. I must show my boss and my boss's boss what I can do so I can advance my career. I must have more likes on Facebook and more followers on Twitter. I need that parking space near the front of the mall. I want that last item at the department store and to drive a new car. I want to live in a bigger house, have the newest iPhone, iPad, and other gadgets. It seems to be all about me.

We think we are individuals who act in the world by ourselves. When we look deeper we realized that so-called "winners" and "losers" didn't appear in a vacuum. So-called "winners" were most often given numerous privileges and teachers that helped them get there, while so-called "losers" were most often plagued with disadvantages and few, if any, positive role models. We seem to act independently. We think we do not need each other, and we act as if we are the only ones on this planet.

Just imagine how much more we can accomplish if we operate in a nondual manner! Imagine how much better the world will be if each one of us incorporates this nondual thinking into our life styles. The Golden Rule, "Do to others, what you would have them do to you," is an inherently nondual statement. It implies intimate connection with, not separation from, the other.

I think we need to take this a step further. We are one with the Earth and everything on it.

This includes soil, waters, plants, trees, bushes, flowers, mountains, air, animals on land and in the sea. We cannot exclude anything. What we do impacts them. And their functioning impacts us.

"Each one of us is a stone on the mosaic that reveals the face of God."[104] Each stone on the face of God needs to shine with its own unique color. Each stone on the face of God needs to express its God-given beauty. The soil needs to remain fresh and fertile and abounding with worms. Plants, trees, bushes, flowers need to grow and flourish for the world to see, for artists to paint, to oxygenate the air, and provide homes and food for insect life. The mountains need to share their beauty, grandeur, and majesty. The air needs to be clean and clear to allow humans and animals to breathe. We exhale carbon dioxide for green life while the green life in return provides us with our oxygen. Tiny ocean plants called phytoplankton contribute 50 to 85 percent of the oxygen in the Earth's atmosphere. We need each other!

Jesus: Nondual Thinker

Jesus conducted Himself in a nondual manner. John 15:5 states, "I am the vine; you are the branches. Those who abide in me and I in them bear much fruit, because apart from me you can do nothing."

We are all in God and God is in us. This means we are all interconnected with one another too. If we maintain this posture, we will act differently. We will bear much different fruit. We will learn to love our neighbor as ourselves (Mark 12:31)—because after all, our neighbor is an extension of our self. When we love our neighbor we love ourselves.

When we put on the mind of Christ, we act differently (Philippians 2:5). We realize that there is enough for everyone. We no longer feel the need to compete with a co-worker. Instead, we help a co-worker succeed. We show him how to do a task that he struggles with. When he is behind and needs some help to catch up, we stop and ask him what tasks we can complete for him. He has an important presentation. We review and listen to the key points he plans to make. We help him tweak his handout and verbal presentation. In other words, we drop the "us and them" mentality, the "me against the world" outlook. Jesus models what this looks like. For Jesus there is no longer "them." There is only "us." It is a whole different way of being in the world.

If I see a hungry woman, I buy her a meal; I don't question whether she really deserves it or not. I don't argue with another's person's point of view; instead, I listen to hear what she has to say. I don't rush to express my opinion. I ask myself, *What can I learn?* I might come to realize that her way makes more sense or I might see an angle that I hadn't thought about before.

My child has just disobeyed a house rule. If I am operating from a nondualist position, I don't yell, but instead, I talk to my child. I explain that he has disobeyed. I tell him it is not okay. I let him know that I love him but if he does it again, there will be a consequence. I might ask him what he could have done differently. Does he understand why his action was inappropriate? I include him in the discussion. I listen to his point of view. I root my actions in compassion. These actions are rooted in nondual thinking. They come from the heart.

Our dualistic mindset is reinforced all of our lives. Most of us live our entire lives in a dualistic manner because we have been heavily scripted from day one. We never leave the dualistic stage. We can transition from dualistic thinking to nondual thinking, yet it takes unlearning most of what we know and starting over.

Centering Prayer: Path to Nondual Thinking

The silence of centering prayer is the portal to the Divine. During silent prayer we put on the Mind of Christ. We die to self. We die to individualism. We shed thoughts that lead to comparison, competition, judgment, splitting the field. We let go and open to the "mind of Christ" (Philippians 2:5).

What is the Mind of Christ? It is a state of mind where we realize that there is no separation between God and us. We also comprehend that no real separation exists between humans. We realize that we are all a larger unity, that separation is an illusion of the ego. One way to visualize this is to think of each person on earth as an individual cell in a large body. Obviously, if a group of cells becomes diseased it affects the whole. Likewise, healthy groups of cells can cause a chain reaction of healing. Like body cells cooperating with one another, we can love and support each other. We can learn from and listen to each other. As the Body of Christ (1 Corinthians 12:12–21), we care for each member of the body.

This is what centering prayer does. Each time we sit in silence, we die to self and open to the Mind of Christ. Slowly over time, dualistic scripting loses its chokehold on us. We become more open to the moment as it rises, without feeling the need to analyze and label everything.

Upgrade Our Operating System

I listened to Cynthia Bourgeault discuss nondual thinking in her audio tape, *Encountering the Wisdom Jesus*.[105] Cynthia mentions that there is no small self. It is a mirage. That is not who I am.

And yet I continue to think I need to be in my small self. I often live from its egoic operating system. My ability to reflect often gets coopted by the ego and perpetuates more binary either/or thinking. To move beyond my inherent attachment to ego-based thoughts is no small order. It takes years, usually decades.

But it is possible. Jesus says that we can upgrade our operating system—and when we do, life can get a whole lot better as we gradually move toward a nondual operating system. In this system, we drop the mind into the heart. The heart picks up reality in a deeper way. It picks up reality by intuition. The heart has a sense of unity. The field is not divided. There is harmony. There is no separation. It is a whole new way of seeing. It is a nondual state.

The nondual state is where compassion and love flow best. To enter this state, we repent of our self-centeredness. We vow to reorient ourselves so Christ is in the center. Then we are capable of a Larger Mind. We go beyond our little mind and enter the Larger Mind that sees from the eyes of the heart. I love the point that Cynthia makes that we need to fry our mental socket. We need a new way to see and be: nondual (Mark 12:31, Matthew 5:44, 10:39, 20:16). This is the gospel!

How do we enter and put on the nondual mind? Personally, I put on the nondual mind via my centering-prayer practice. I believe, though, that any type of contemplative practice that slows you down so you die to self and open to the mind of Christ will work. Silence, lectio divina, centering prayer, Christian meditation, labyrinth walking, writing, and art, to name only a few, are contemplative practices that help us die to self and put on the mind of Christ.

Dangers of Dualism

N. T. Wright makes this very direct point about the dangers of dualism: "Armageddon is coming, so who cares about acid rain or third world debt? That is the way of dualism: it is a radically anti-creation viewpoint."[106]

Dualistic thinking can be very dangerous. We focus on what is in it for me. We become greedy and are more concerned with how much money we can make. We don't worry about our world, other countries, and struggling nations. "Me first" and "America first" become mantras. We don't worry about the environment and greenhouse gasses. We don't worry about the living standards and lack of schooling for girls in developing nations. We don't worry about the homeless that struggle among us.

Nondual Thinking Is Contagious

Jesus tells us there is a new way. "Watch Me," He says. "Listen to Me. Learn from Me. Take this parable and play with it. See what you discover." Sometimes, Jesus simply asks questions. He wants people to learn for themselves. Often the best way to teach is to ask questions and let the student do her own thinking.

Jesus was a master of nondual thinking and teaching, and He shared this vision. This nondual vision is key to God's new creation. It is the power of God flowing through humanity. It is the attainment of our potential as an individual yet an integral part of the whole. It is the end of human suffering caused by alienation and isolation.

Is a nondual world attainable? It seems unlikely. However, it is possible when we build it one person at a time. We each have our part to play. When I see another person do his or her part, suddenly I see a family do it. I then see neighbors participate. I see it move from neighbors to a small community. It has power. It seems to grow legs and move. We see it in action when we witness a community work together to help each other. Someone is sick and the community bands together to provide meals and care for the children of the sick. We see it when a member of the community loses a loved one. Cards are sent. Food is brought to the person who mourns. Flowers are sent. Kind words are spoken. Sometimes no words are spoken; friends just sit with the mourners in their loss.

Every day we can look to see where we can advance this Kingdom of God. When we do, it becomes contagious. Others want to join in.

Nondual Thinking in the Workplace

As we grow up, we seem to lose our ability to be nondual thinkers. This is a byproduct of our schools and our workplaces. In school, it is more about how to get good grades on the test than how to help each other. We learn to not be present in the moment. We memorize. We do what it takes to get good grades. It is more important to learn how to take the college entrance exam than to show compassion. We are ranked. This competition continues in college. "I need to graduate with as high a GPA as possible," we say to ourselves. "I want the best employers to recruit and hire me. I want a high salary." We graduate and enter the workplace. The competition continues. "How can I outperform my peers? How can I shine? I need to lead. My bonus is on the line. My year-end merit increase is dependent upon how I do in comparison to my peers. If I land at the bottom of the rankings, I will not get a bonus or merit increase. I might even get pushed out of the company." This is not the Kingdom of God.

We need to bring the Kingdom of God into our workplaces. It is possible, but it will take place one person at a time. It is not about what I can accomplish; it is about what we can accomplish together. It is not about how to outshine my peers; it is about how I can help my peer also be successful. It is how we can perform as a complimentary team. Ralph is excellent with Internet technology but not great at public presentation; Susan is an excellent presenter but lacks the IT skills—so we put them together to create a presentation better than they could have come up with on their own. We can help each other succeed.

When individual personalities shine and at the same time are recognized as valuable members and contributors to a team culture, people do not need to conform. We need to let each person's diverse gifts flourish in the workplace. We can build this Kingdom one person at a time, inside the workplace and outside.

The Unity of the Incarnation

The incarnation of Christ is proof of unity. The eternal and the finite came together in Jesus. In each one of us as well the eternal and the finite come together. Often, though, we just do not let the two meet.

Our inner divinity and our humanity are one. That is who we are. They both need each other. Our humanity is an expression of our inner divinity. We are all at different stages. Some of us think we are only human and identify mostly with the messes in our lives. Some of us are at the other extreme. We think we are divine and emphasize how blessed we are. We think we are better than others and compete with others to prove it. Instead, the two need to be in balance.

When we let our inner divinity and our humanity meet, we realize that we are in life together with everyone else—that everyone is blessed and everyone has messes. We realize that we don't need to waste so much energy on competition. We need to express our unique inner divinity, creativity, compassion.

We are all interrelated. We are not separate, and there is no separation between God and humans, aside from the divide we create in our minds. There is no separation between humans and humans either, aside from the divide in our minds. We are all in this interdependent life together. There is enough for everyone.

The problem is not God's abundance. The problem is our human distribution systems. There is enough food to feed the world; we just don't prioritize equitable distribution. We don't need to fight over resources; we need to share the resources. This world will change as more and more people realize that their inner divinity and humanity are not separate, and neither are we separate from our neighbor and her needs.

There is a dynamism between divinity and humanity, Creator and creature, absolute and relative, immortal and mortal. I experience the Divine Presence during centering prayer, and then I aim to bring that Presence into my human actions. We need Divine Presence, immersed in stillness and silence, to balance our hyperactivity. And God needs more humans to embody Divine Presence in their actions.

My journey has been about embodying the Divine Presence in my human actions. The more I see that dynamism at work in God and in the Gospels, the more that dynamism shows up in my life. First we have to see the two together in Jesus. Then there is hope that we will put the two together in ourselves. If I think that God is up there and I am down here and never the two shall meet, then we will never put the two together. We will never think and act holistically (nondualistically).

Everything Is Connected

God died when Jesus died. The eternal became finite. At the resurrection, however, the human Jesus rose—and the finite became eternal. Death did not have the final say. Death is in life and life is in death. They form a seamless whole.

This changes how I look at things. If life and death are not separate but part of a singular dynamic, what about all the parts of my life? My family, friends, workplace, community, supermarket, the park, recreational activities, places where I volunteer, workout, commute—none of it is separated; all of it is connected. What I do and say impacts the whole.

Nothing is separate. My thoughts that I am alone are a mirage. When our inner divinity meets and begins to work with our humanity, life becomes enchanted again. We become like children playing in the creek bed for hours, losing all track of time.

• • • • • • • • • • • • • • • • • • • •

Questions for Reflection and Discussion

1. What are some examples of nondual thinking?

2. Do you think Jesus was a nondual thinker? Why or why not?

3. How can silent prayer be a path to nondual thinking?

4. Do you agree with Cynthia Bourgeault that the heart picks up reality in a deeper way? Why or why not?

5. What does it mean to operate from your heart?

6. What are dangers of dual thinking?

Chapter 12

. . . .

THE MYSTERY AND PARADOX OF JESUS

. . . .

The truth is that we spend our lives
in the centrifuge of paradox.

—**Joan Chittister** [107]

The Jesus Paradox is Christianity's
mystic core.

—**Amos E. Smith** [108]

esus is at once God and human. This truth, referred to as the Jesus Paradox, reminds me that God loves us. God chose to incarnate in human form. She chose to commune with us and become one of us, sharing in all or our limitations and sufferings.

Jesus did not write a book. He was the human "Word" of God in action. He was God's book, so to speak.

If we open to the Jesus Paradox, we are better able to open to all of the beauty around us. We do not need to understand everything to enjoy it. We ask God, *What future actions should we take as a result of this paradox?* The Jesus Paradox means we do not limit ourselves. It opens us to unlimited possibilities. We have widened our lens. We no longer have tunnel vision. The Jesus Paradox is a life-long journey to discover both the historical Jesus and the Christ of faith.

In *Did God Kill Jesus?*, Tony Jones wrote, "This event, the crucifixion, on which all of cosmic history pivots, forever changed both us and God."[109] Many people will argue that God cannot change. He is the same yesterday, today and in the future. I believe that the essence of God is unchangeable—and yet God changed when He entered time and became one of us. Tony goes on to say, that God learned, and I believe this was a new experience for God. He learned what it was to be human. The Incarnation changed God and us. Through Jesus, Divinity was humbled and humanity was glorified.[110]

In Jesus, God went from pity to genuine empathy for the human condition. Finally, God came to understand us after becoming one of us. In human form, He experienced the full range of our humanity. God felt extreme fear, despair, physical pain, and humiliation.

On the cross Jesus, cried, "My God, my God, why have you forsaken me?" (Psalm 22:1). So God experienced the absence of God on the cross.

Jurgen Moltmann wrote, "'God was in Christ, reconciling the world to himself (2 Corinthians 5:19). If God the Father was in Christ, the Son, this means that Christ's sufferings are God's sufferings too, and then God too experiences death on the cross."[111] This is truly a paradox that reveals how far God will go. It reveals how much God loves humanity. God became one of us, suffered like one of us, died like one of us. God experienced the absence of God.

Like many, I have experienced God's absence. There are days when I wonder where God is. This is not the end of the story, though. God cannot die. God was resurrected. Death was conquered. God's love for humanity has overcome death.

Jesus emptied Himself of His Divinity (Philippians 2:7)—and yet this humility made Him more Divine, not less. This is what Cyril of Alexandria and other early theologians called "the economy of the incarnation,"[112] whereby Jesus' emptying produced not a subtraction of His nature but an addition. "The Son of God," taught the early Church Fathers, "was made human that we might be made God."

Jesus experienced all the highs and lows of life and death, but at the same time, He did not relinquish His Divinity. He died—and then was raised again after three days. Just when you think He is completely human (so human that He surrendered to death), His Divinity is revealed. There is creative tension between His Divinity and humanity throughout the Gospels. In Jesus, God nursed His mother, God cried, God died. Likewise in Jesus, God healed terminal illnesses, miraculously fed multitudes, and rose from the dead.

When are Jesus' actions Divine? When are His actions human? It is a paradox. It's okay that I do not understand this. I don't have to understand. I believe it. I will open myself to this paradox and see where it takes me. I grapple with the meaning, mystery, and beauty of this paradox.

The Fruit of Centering Prayer Is a Paradox

During centering prayer, we let go of all thoughts, emotions, bodily sensations. We let go of trying to let go. We let things be. We have nothing to prove. We let go of the need to know why we feel our thoughts and emotions. We let go of the need to know God's ultimate name or identity. When we let go, paradoxically we are most open. You would think that letting go would create a vacuum or a lack. Yet the opposite is true. It creates a receptive buoyant fullness. Centering prayer, like the Incarnation, has its own paradoxical economy.

In our consumeristic society, we are accustomed to thinking that if we acquire another possession we will be fulfilled on some level. Yet often the opposite is true. After we buy something, we experience buyer's remorse; perhaps we are saddled with monthly payments that become burdensome, or maybe we realize that whatever this new thing is, it's just one more piece of clutter. Centering prayer teaches us that emptiness is fullness and that acquisitiveness is often folly. And the greatest achievement is to be able to say, "I have everything I need."

When we let go of all thoughts, there are no barriers between God and us. It is now God's move. God might choose to act!

Once when I was in an open receptive place after prayer, suddenly my surroundings became brighter, sharper, clearer. The Energy of Life infused everything. A gentle breeze brushed across my skin. The sky was a beautiful light blue. My son Josh smiled each time he rode his bike past me. Pure joy radiated from him. My daughter Gabbie continued to talk to me while we threw a ball back and forth. I was calm, at peace. I was more present than I have ever felt before. I did not reflect on the past. I did not plan upcoming events. I did not worry about the future. I just was in the present moment. I was enveloped in the fullness of God, surrounded by God, in God. In that moment, I was in God, in whom I "live and move and have my being" (Acts 17:28).

Then the moment ended. I was back. I did not ask to be placed into that other realm, and I did not ask to be removed from it. It just happened. So I waited with a posture of openness to the eternal revelation of God's presence.

My wait lasted until a Sunday when I was in New York City. I arrived a day early for a work meeting on Monday. After my arrival at the hotel, I decided to walk the city. I love to walk the streets of New York City! I saw a beautiful park and decided to sit outside in Union Square.

Suddenly, I felt Life all around me, loud and vibrant. I was overwhelmed and amazed at the same time. I felt connected to everyone in the crowded park. I felt connected to the ground and the trees. I felt connected to all of the sounds.

I believe God wanted me to see the power of Life. She wanted me to experience Life with all my senses: sounds, aromas, tastes, beauty, texture. I surmise that it was so powerful because a sixth sense was involved: my spiritual sense. The Divine elevated and magnified the five other senses. After about thirty minutes, I arose. I called a friend to share the experience. I explained that most people might have thought I was crazy, but I felt Life vibrate all around me and it was beautiful—and at the same time it overwhelmed and drained me.

To let go is truly a paradox. It opens me to the powerful presence of the Divine! When I am empty, I am full. When I die, I live.

Contradictions of Life

Henri Nouwen wrote:

The many contradictions in our lives—such as being home while feeling homeless, being busy while feeling bored, being popular while feeling lonely, being believers while feeling many doubts—can frustrate, irritate, and even discourage us. They make us feel that we are never fully present. Every door that opens for us makes us see how many more doors are closed.

But there is another response. These same contradictions can bring us in touch with a deeper longing, for the fulfillment of a desire that lives beneath all desires and that only God can satisfy.[113]

I can relate to what Henri says. Sometimes at both work and home, I am busy, and at the same time I am bored. At home, my wife and I divide and conquer the household chores. Dishes need to be cleaned, groceries purchased, laundry washed and folded, meals cooked, house cleaned. The kids need to be driven to appointments and to and from their friends' houses to play. At work, phone calls and emails beckon. Daily tasks need to be completed. Sometimes, I don't feel fulfilled. Does what I do make a difference? Does it matter to anyone? Does it matter to God?

What do I do with this boredom? Nouwen suggests that I pay attention to the friction. God is in the friction. What can it teach me? I can let God lead me to, through, and out the other side of the friction.

I can view the friction in another way as well. What can I see that I never noticed before? Perhaps I can see something that changes my boredom to excitement. I also recognize when God nudges me to make a change. Perhaps there are tasks that I need to stop so I can do new things. At home, this might mean I switch tasks with my wife or even hire someone to do them. At work, I can evaluate if these tasks are still necessary. I might even consider a new role within my company. I won't discover any of these things without friction.

Friction is to be embraced. It leads me to God. He is in the friction. When I let go and live into that friction, a freshness is injected into my routines. I may be doing the same routine, but I think about it in new ways. There is space and exploration whereas before there was dullness. It's hard to explain, but centering prayer transforms me from a dull expert to an inquisitive beginner.

Life Is a Paradox

Christine Valters Painter wrote:

> However, there is a paradox that comes with these realizations. While we must venture far to find our "true self," it is always with us. I

have found I can embark on a long journey that often takes many years to find that I am back where I started. It is here that I am happy.[114]

At work, I was an individual contributor for the first ten years. This meant I had assigned duties with no one reporting to me directly. I came in and performed my assigned tasks. After ten years, I ventured into managing people for another ten years. I enjoyed this experience. I wanted to help co-workers see the potential I saw in them, and I enjoyed pushing people to do things they did not know they could achieve. I liked to help people, but I began to feel bored and unfulfilled. I felt that I had stopped my growth. I am now an individual contributor again and have been so the last eight years. I no longer have anyone who reports to me directly. I feel much better. This is who I am. It is always who I was. I needed to be a people manager to realize who I always was.

This is just one example. We have all taken long journeys only to discover what we wanted, who we truly are, is in front of us.

The Gospels Are Paradox

In the New Testament, we see Jesus making paradoxical statements. Matthew 10:39 is just one example: "Those who find their life will lose it, and those who lose their life for my sake will find it." Jesus was not talking about a physical death but rather a mental death. He wanted to raise us to a new level of consciousness, where we let go of our egos. Our egos judge people. They say, "I am always right." They insist that the world is divided into "my way" and "your way." Our egos live in fear. They do not want to be offended. They want to win.

Jesus says there is another way. We need to transcend our egos if we truly want to see and live. When I let my ego die, it is then that I truly live. I see other points of view. I see that I don't need to win. I see that there is enough for everyone. I see that we are all connected. We can fight and compete—or we can share and live together in community. We can work together to make our family, community, church, or monastery a place where everyone has an opportunity to live an abundant life (John 10:10). Every day, I remind myself that I am not an individual; I am part of the community. I am part of the Body of Christ.

Luke 6:38 states, "Give, and it will be given to you . . . for the measure you give will be the measure you get back." Life is not about what I can get. It is about what I can give. Paradoxically, we find the most joy when we give.

Laurence Freeman wrote:

His [Jesus'] continuing presence within the absence created by his death is the gospel's essential message. His disappearance in death and the absence of his visible form are the conditions of his presence in the Spirit. His absence is a necessary aspect for this presence.[115]

This is certainly not to be expected but continues to this day some two thousand years after the death of Jesus. Something wonderful happened. In His death, His Spirit was released and continues to act in this world through each of us. Jesus needed to die to live. He now lives in each of us. He is expressed through each of us.

Centering Prayer Is a Paradox

Richard Rohr reminds us, "To be a Christian is to objectively know that we share the same identity that Jesus enjoyed as both human and divine, which is what it means to 'follow' him."[116] I will best follow Jesus when I too recognize that I am both human and divine. My humanity is best expressed or lived as an outpouring of my divinity. How do I live from my divinity? Through centering prayer.

My inner spirit is the seed from which my human actions sprout. My centering prayer, along with my times of pause and prayer throughout the day, water my inner spirit. As I water my inner spirit, its roots grow deeper. My actions emerge from these roots, but the roots will shrivel without daily watering. My daily waterings are centering prayer, silent pauses, and verbal prayer.

I connect to my inner divinity with centering prayer. This is the place deep within where God resides, a place that knows only love. It will remain hidden within me unless I penetrate it with prayer, unless from time to time I take a silent pause before I take an action I will later regret.

Within silence is Love. Love wants to leave this silent space and flow into the world. Jesus' human actions sprang from His times of silent prayer—and like Jesus, my human actions spring from my times of silent prayer and silent pauses.

Jesus Is the Template for Paradox

Not only is Jesus human; He is also Divine. However, we need to qualify this. What part of Jesus is Divine? What part of Jesus is human? This question cannot be answered. Jesus is both.

To state that Jesus is only human diminishes who He is. To state that Jesus is only God equally diminishes who He is. He is at once both human and Divine. Let me also explain what I mean by Divine. Jesus is not merely a divine being. Jesus is God in the flesh. Jesus is the manifestation of God in human form. Or as Brian Zahnd likes to say, "Jesus is what God has to say."[117]

We do not need to understand this. Our human minds want to put Jesus in one category. Jesus is human, end of story. Jesus is God, end of story. Yet, when it comes to Jesus, reductionist either/or binaries won't do. I suggest that we let Jesus be both—and open to the mystery.

Let me also suggest that a consistent, daily centering prayer practice will help birth human actions that over time reflect actions that Jesus the human being would do. We learn about these actions in the Gospels: acts of compassion, forgiveness, and inclusion. Our actions over time, as we continue a centering-prayer practice, will reflect the fruits of the Spirit: love, joy, peace, patience, kindness, goodness, faithfulness, gentleness, self-control (Galatians 5:22).

What Do We Do with the Jesus Paradox?

I don't think people know how to handle the Jesus Paradox. Personally, I dive into the Jesus

Paradox via my centering prayer. Silence opens me to paradox.

As Paul shared in his message, "You are God's temple" (1 Corinthians 3:16), but many people don't think of themselves as divine beings. For a long time, I didn't. We fail to see or accept that the light is in us too; we don't understand how much this can change our lives. We fail to understand how much God loves us. We fail to understand that God's love has been poured out for us in Jesus, not just in apostolic days, but today. Disciplined silences, sitting with God in centering prayer, can open our eyes. Jesus continues to heal the blind, from the time of the Gospels through to the present day.

Silence is difficult. Silence slows us down. It opens us to paradox. Silence opens us to God in Christ, who loves us more than we can comprehend!

• •

Questions for Reflection and Discussion

1. What does it mean to you when Jesus is referred to as at once God and human?

2. How do you define paradox?

3. What things do you think about as being a paradox?

4. Do you believe that you are made in the image of God and at the same time are a human? What does it mean for you to be both divine and human?

5. Are you comfortable with just not knowing?

6. In what ways is life a paradox?

Chapter 13

. . . .

COSMIC CHRIST, INFINITE WORD

. . . .

In the beginning was the Word.

—John 1:1

Before Abraham was, I am.

—Jesus[118]

Leonard Sweet and Frank Viola state, "Christ is so large that no search party in the universe can explore an iota of His infinite depths."[119] They are talking about the Christ that existed from eternity, eons before Jesus of Nazareth walked the earth. Jesus was a man who existed at one point in time. The Christ, on the other hand, existed from all of eternity. Some theologians refer to this eternal Being as the Cosmic Christ or the Universal Christ. To scratch the surface of this Cosmic Christ, I read Richard Rohr and Ilia Delio. I also took a look at what the Apostle Paul had to say.

Incarnations of Christ

The Greeks called the eternal Christ the *Logos* ("Word" in English), which is the organizing principle out of which the universe emerges. Richard Rohr tells us Christ is the eternal union of matter and Spirit from the beginning of time.[120] This gives us a better sense of the Cosmic Christ. The Cosmic Christ is as small as the smallest particle and as vast as the largest planet. The Cosmic Christ is on the move. It constantly creates.

The Cosmic Christ decided to reveal itself 14.6 billion years ago with the Big Bang. We can call this the first incarnation. Four billion years ago was another incarnation. The Earth was formed. There was light, land, vegetation, creatures on land and sea. Then, two thousand years ago, was the human incarnation of God: Jesus of Nazareth.

This is an exquisitely patient God. An enormous amount of time has passed to get to this point.

So what does this mean? This means Christ is in everything. Unfortunately, we do not live as though this is true. We have wars. Racism is rampant. We pollute our planet. We think and act like individuals who live separate lives. Yet as Paul reminds us, we are the Body of Christ (1 Corinthians 12:27). We are each part of something much bigger than just us. We each have our part to play.

Paul wrote:

> For just as the body is one and has many members, and all the members of the body, though many, are one body, so it is with Christ. For in the one Spirit we were all baptized into one body—Jews or Greeks, slaves or free—and we were all made to drink of one Spirit. (1 Corinthians 12:12–13)

In the same chapter, Paul goes on to say, "As it is, there are many members, yet one body. The eye cannot say to the hand, 'I have no need of you,' nor again the head to the feet, 'I have no need of you'" (verses 20–21) Paul concludes: "Now you are the body of Christ and individually members of it" (verse 27).

I have my part to play. You have yours. We need to work together, not against each other. The world we live in does not act as though it is the Body of Christ. The corporate world certainly does not act as if it is Christ's Body. It competes. It says: "I am better than you." "I can beat you." "I don't need you." "You are expendable." "I can eliminate you." "I can replace you."

We do the same thing in our churches, social organizations, government, and even within our families. We forget we are Christ's Body. Those who understand this reality need to teach others. It is best taught by our actions. It is revealed in how we conduct ourselves at home, with our friends, at work, in the community.

My actions impact others. For example, at work, if I decide not to come in, someone else has to do my work plus their work. I have impacted them. Their day has changed. If I make an angry remark at someone, I have impacted them. I might feel better, while they might feel hurt. They might not trust me anymore. My friendship with them might be changed or lost. In the natural world, squirrels deliver scat at the base of trees that have the specific nutrients the tree roots need to survive. And tree root systems line the banks of rivers, which keep the waters from flooding the land. These brief examples reveal how we are all connected.

Silence is a universal phenomenon—an experience I share with all other living things. A silent pause reminds me that we are all connected. Silence allows me to release my hurtful intentions. I am freed of them. I leave them in the silence and reemerge from the silence a new creature.

Silence is often the best action. It reconnects us with our true self. Our true self does not want to respond with hurtful and angry actions. Our true self knows we are all the Body of Christ. Our true self knows how to respond from a place of compassion. Silence restores our sense of interconnection and interdependence with the larger Body of Christ (which extends out into the entire universe). The Cosmic Christ is in the silence, in the numerous cells that form one body, in the primordial Word that existed before time and that brought all things into being.

Paul's Theology

The synoptic Gospels are stories about the historical Jesus, while the epistles written by Paul describe his experience of the eternal Christ Mystery. Paul never met Jesus—and yet he wrote roughly two-thirds of the New Testament. Some key Paulian themes resonate with me.

We all live and move and have our being in God (Acts 17:28). We are never separate from God. We can't be (Romans 8:38). My life participates in God. Our bodies are the temple of God (1 Corinthians 3:16, 6:19). The Christ lives in each one of us (Romans 8:10). For Paul this is the great mystery that we most often fail to see.

Paul's experience of the resurrected Jesus is the root of his theology. After the Damascus Road experience, Paul went to Arabia. We do not know how long he remained there, but we do know that he left Arabia a new creation (Ephesians 4:22). He had put on the "Mind of Christ." Paul had become a mystic, a nondual thinker. The Christ that is within all initially did not make sense to Paul. He did not think of himself as a Jesus persecutor until his eyes were opened to the Christ Mystery. Then he saw the Christ in himself and in everything. He now understood what Jesus meant when He asked Paul, "Why do you persecute me?" (Acts 9:4). Paul now realized that what he did to others he did to Jesus the Christ (Matthew 25:40).

My entry into the Mind of Christ is centering prayer. That is why centering prayer is a daily practice for me. Every day I put on the Mind of Christ (Philippians 2:5).

Discover Christ Anew

Ilia Delio wrote that, "Every age must discover Christ anew."[121] She further explained, "But to say Jesus is the Christ means that he is the long awaited fullness of God's presence."[122] Ilia reminds us that Jesus is the Christ, but Christ is more than Jesus alone. Christ encompasses the whole cosmos. Christ is the "in the beginning . . . Word" (John 1:1). Creation reveals the infinite love of the Word in its own way. There is nothing created that does not have a divine dignity to it. All of creation reflects God and Christ in some way (John 1: 1–3).

My centering-prayer practice grounds me and connects me to the Christ Mystery. I view each day as an opportunity to discover Christ anew. Centering prayer helps me see Christ in all I see: people, trees, plants, waters, mountains, sky, stars. I am surrounded. When my eyes open to the Word, I am ambushed and pummeled by Presence and grace. I also realize that I am a work in progress. I need to mature. I need to treat the Christ much better than I do (Matthew 25:40).

Ilia wrote, "While the fullness of God's love is reveled in Jesus, what happened to Jesus must happen to us."[123] What does this mean? It means it is not enough to understand that Jesus was God incarnate. I need to go further. Jesus was crucified, died, and raised from the dead. I too must die and rise again. I must let go of the little Rich who is afraid, angry, boastful, jealous, insecure. Little Rich is an individual who thinks the world is created for him to conquer. This Rich must die. When he does, a new Rich can emerge. A new Rich can be resurrected.

The resurrected Rich is not afraid. This Rich may get angry but does not say hurtful things to others. This Rich feels no need to boast. This Rich is not jealous but is happy when others achieve their goals. This Rich is confident because he knows who he is. He knows his body is the temple of God in Christ. He knows the Christ Mystery resides within him and vies for unique expression. This is the Rich I want to be!

The death and resurrection we experience alongside Christ is no fabrication or yarn. It is no psychological concept. Back in the seventeenth century, George Fox, for example, suffered three years in an open-roof prison in Nottingham, England, where his joints swelled and he nearly died. Although he did not physically die, this was certainly a "death experience"—and it was followed by resurrection. Soon after his release, Quaker Meeting Houses blossomed throughout England, thanks both to George's work and the grace of God. All of Christ's followers through the ages have also had their death and resurrection experiences—all of them visceral and unmistakable.

The Mystery of God's Strength

Within you is power and love (Psalm 62:11–12). Within each one of us are powerful strengths, abilities, and skills. Some of us are blessed with gifts of writing, teaching, listening, drawing, painting. Others are blessed with gifts of speaking, leading, analyzing, organizing, patience.

Once we discover our sometimes hidden gifts, we must act! However, we must temper the power of our actions with love. The two work together. Power without love is selfish. Our power is best used when rooted in love. Actions rooted in love are powerful!

Saint Paul's sole intention was to build up the early churches. He had no idea that his writings would outlive him for thousands of years and become canonized in the New Testament. His motivation was to love the early churches in Christ's name. This love galvanized early Christianity. The love at the root of Paul's actions was what made them so powerful and transformative for generations to come.

When the gifts God has given us are rooted in love, they can move mountains.

The Cosmic Christ Creates

Laurence Freeman wrote:

> The Cosmic Christ is not a universal archetype projected onto the historical Jesus but the core of Jesus' identity revealed in the way history and geography were transcended in the Resurrection.[124]

Yes, this Cosmic Christ is at the core of Jesus. This Cosmic Christ is also at the core of our beings. It is at the core of all that exists (John 1:1–5). It is what causes us to burst forth with life. All of creation reflects the Word's dynamic and creative beauty and ongoing expansion.

The Cosmic Christ bursts forth and expresses itself in atoms, molecules, communities, and galaxies! Jesus the human died. Jesus the Christ transcended death. The Cosmic Christ cannot die. The Cosmic Christ always was and is, past, present, future. It is eternal with no beginning, middle, or end (Hebrews 13:8).

We humans have a difficult time understanding transcendence. The *Free Dictionary* defines *transcend*: "to pass beyond the limits of (a category or conception), for instance, to be greater than, as in quality or intensity; surpass, to exist above and independent of (material experience or the universe)."

Humans tend to think of things as finite. The Cosmic Christ is not finite. The eternal Word is infinite and has no boundaries or limits. The creative Word that has existed from the beginning of time is impossible to measure or calculate (John 1:1, Genesis 1:3). The infinite Word is as small as the particles within an atom and as vast as the expanding universe. The Cosmic Christ is revealed and expressed when Spirit and matter combine. We don't need to understand it; all we can do is trust. Its infinite creativity, resilience, and energy abound around us.

God's Kingdom

Christ was the personification of the Kingdom of God at a point of time in the person of Jesus. This Kingdom of God is not once and done, however. It had ramifications for all time. Its ripple effects are felt today when someone turns their world around with Christ as their exemplar. Bethlehem two thousand years ago was ground zero—but the effects of that blast are still felt today.

The blast of the Incarnation moves in all directions. It is completed through people—and through animals, birds, trees, plants, the Earth, the mountains, waters, other planets, and the furthest reaches of the universe that have no end. The blast of the Incarnation put God's Kingdom in motion. The Kingdom of God is a new reality that is reborn in numerous surprising ways in every generation. Its ripple effects will continue to be felt in untold startling ways for generations.

Everything has a reason and point for existence. When organisms are in alignment and true to their nature, they reveal and express God's Kingdom. They share in and point to God's Kingdom. They spread God's Kingdom.

The Kingdom Is Love

The Kingdom of God is love in action. It is the spread of love. Love needs to find the absence of love and fill it. Just like water gravitates to the lowest point, so too Christ gravitates to the poor, lepers, extortionists, prostitutes (Mark 2:17, Luke 5:31). A lonely woman sits in church and is joined by a smiling face. A homeless man is hungry and is provided a sandwich. A community welcomes a stranger for who he is and as he is with no judgment. A family cannot pay their electric bill as a result of unexpected medical bills, and a member of the community pays the bill for them. A man toils through boot camp with his alcohol addiction an untold secret—yet he leans on his faith, reads a psalm every night, and somehow finds the interior resources and grit to pull through. These are all the Kingdom of God. They all embody Christ.

The Christ Is Coming to Be

In an article in *America Magazine*, Ilia Delio, states, "This universe is holy because it is grounded in the Word of God. It is Christ, the living one, who is coming to be."[125] The Christ boldly acts, creates, evolves. The ever-creative Word is a constant outpouring of love. It must be. Look around. You can see the Word in action. It is a human baby, a newborn calf, a flower that pushes through the topsoil. It is the sunrise as a new day bursts forth. It is children who light up a room with their laughter and play.

> I am the light that is over them all. I am the All: the All has come forth from me and the All has returned to me. Cleave a piece of wood: I am there. Raise up a stone, and you will find me there.[126]

This verse from the Gospel of Thomas compels us to sanctify life, for life is holy. Christ is within it.

Love and Creation vigorously move and unfold. God wants us to revel in them. She also wants us to participate. We open ourselves and let the Christ act through us, so that we become the hands and feet of this Love and Creation. We become its voice.

The Christ of Our Faith

After the Resurrection, the Cosmic Christ came alive in the early Jewish disciples. It continues to be alive to this day and act through each one of us.

Everything we touch embodies the Cosmic Christ. When the veil of prime-time drivel and cotton candy is lifted, we see: everything is holy. This changes how we treat each other and the Earth we inhabit.

Jesus was the human incarnation of God in a single point of time. This time lasted some thirty-three years. We learn about this human Jesus in the Gospels. We see His human actions on display. We see Him love and heal. We see Him eat and dine with the marginalized. No one is excluded.

Jesus is also the infinite Word (John 1:1). He is the Christ whom I have been trying to draw out, yet ultimately when it comes to the mystery of the Word (singular), words (plural) fail us. Christ is the underlying unity that mystics stammer about. "In the beginning was the Word" (John 1:1).

We see a human Jesus accept His death on the cross. He chose not to run away. Jesus did not have to go into Jerusalem. He could have played it safe and not entered the city's walls. He could have remained hidden and on the run the rest of His life—but He chose not to do so. He chose a different path, a path of surrender. He was not afraid to walk this path. He challenged us to follow Him.

Jesus was the Christ, the infinite Word, definitively spoken once in time for all to hear, and spoken through the ages through people who put on the Mind of Christ (Philippians 2:5–8).

I will never get my arms around the full meaning and power of Jesus Christ. I will continue to study the Gospels and read biographies and commentaries. I will enter the silence of centering prayer and let the Word reveal itself. When I am steeped in the Divine Presence in stillness and silence, I am steeped in the Word. When I am steeped in the human words and actions of my day, I am a member of Jesus' Body.

Through centering prayer, I participate in the dynamism of the human Jesus and the Divine Christ. I am in the world from a contemplative center. When I do this, my prayer and actions have symmetry and poise and are a reflection of Jesus, the Christ.

Jim Marion wrote, "Jesus is the name of the little human body (personality) in which the vast Christ Consciousness was born."[127] We are all the little bodies in which this vast Christ consciousness can be born. Notice I spelled consciousness with a small "c." We are divine beings with a little "d." Jesus was the Divine being with a big "D." Jesus was God incarnate. Jesus was the Christ Consciousness. We too are the Christ consciousness. We are to put on the Mind of Christ and become new creatures (2 Corinthians 5:17).

I am on a lifelong journey of continuous discovery. I want to continue to discover and mirror the dynamic unity of the human Jesus and the Divine Christ in my prayers and actions.

• • • • • • • • • • • • • • • • • • • •

Questions for Reflection and Discussion

1. What is the Cosmic Christ?

2. Does the Cosmic Christ change how you live, how you think about God?

3. God created the universe some 14 billion years ago. The Earth was created some 4 billion years ago. The human incarnation of God in Jesus was two thousand years ago. What does this tell us about God?

4. Ilia Delio said that every age must discover Christ anew. Do you agree? Why or why not?

5. How can you explore the Christ Mystery?

Chapter 14

. . . .

EMBRACING THE MYSTERY OF JESUS' DYNAMIC UNITY AT WORK IN ME

. . . .

The heart of the Christian spiritual journey
is God's determined will to transmit to us
the maximum of divine light,
life, love and happiness
that we can possibly receive.

—**Thomas Keating**[128]

Daily, I sit with God in Christ. Daily the Word is revealed to me. Daily, I rest in silent prayer and let the Jesus Paradox penetrate deep within my soul. I let it teach me how to live.

Centering prayer teaches me how to rest in the mystery of the Jesus Paradox: the Divinity and humanity of Jesus. I learn how to connect with God, to rest in God's loving arms. I begin to trust and let God act in me. I learn how to be human, how to live in the world.

In order to best live in this world, I continue my centering-prayer practice. I don't practice out of guilt; I do it because I love God. I need this special time each day. It refreshes, grounds, and centers me. As I practice centering prayer, I live from this stable place more and more. My outer world is a reflection of my inner world, centered, grounded, spacious.

Cynthia Bourgeault wrote that toward the beginning of her centering-prayer practice, silence and stillness was a foreign land that she visited. It was a place that she would go to. Now after many years of centering prayer, stillness is a familiar homeland. Now it is where she comes from. It is her center.[129] Instead of being centered in a frantic pace, which is no center at all, I am too now centered within. Silence has become a refuge, a reservoir of renewal that is deepest during prayer times but is accessible to me throughout the day. All I have to do is pause and return to myself, myself united to Christ in prayer.

I am always amazed by the fruits of my centering prayer revealed in my non-silent parts of each day. Silent prayer is a journey into greater dynamism and balance in my life. I need it. I am a better person because of it. It teaches me how to live.

I follow the model of Jesus, who was an activist with a contemplative center. He ministered to the crowds that pressed in on Him. He had compassion on the multitudes. Yet He often retreated by Himself to solitary places to pray (Mark 5:1, Mark 5:24, Luke 5:16, Mark 1:35). Jesus modeled an abundant life of prayer and action in the world. I want to mirror Him as best I can.

I am in touch with the absolute Divinity of Jesus through deep periods of centering prayer. I am also in touch with the relative humanity of Jesus through my non-centering parts of the day. The deep sacred silences remind me that I am blessed. And my waking consciousness throughout the day reminds me of the messiness of my humanity.

Now I can hold contradictions together in creative tension. In so doing, I mirror, in some small way, the transfiguration of Jesus on Mount Tabor and the humiliation of Jesus on the cross. Both are an integral part of my life and journey, and in some small way they both mirror Him, who held it all together from the infinite macrocosm to the finite microcosm. He can hold me together, even when I feel like I'm falling apart. His dynamic unity is fully present in my messes and in my moments of glory.

Centering prayer is the path of abundance I have chosen that embraces the mystery of Jesus' dynamic unity. There are other silent prayer practices, besides centering prayer, and I encourage you to find one that is life-giving to you—but I will continue to practice centering prayer and share it with others. I will not say this is the *only* way. I will encourage others to try it and see what happens. Centering prayer has been so life-giving to me that I cannot help but pass it on. As Basil Pennington wrote:

> If we experience in our own selves the need, the value, and the joy of being in touch with the contemplative dimension of our lives, then is it not incumbent upon us to seek to make this possible for others? "Freely have you received, freely must you give." [130]

I sit with Jesus so I can walk with Jesus!
I hope to share the journey with you.

Questions for Reflection and Discussion

1. Have you tried a contemplative practice such as centering prayer? If not, would you consider doing so now, after having read this book? Why or why not?

2. The silence of centering prayer is rest and trust in God. How does that make you feel?

3. Do you believe that your outer world is a reflection of your inner world? Why or why not?

Endnotes

1. N. T. Wright. *Simply Jesus: A New Vision of Who He Was, What He Did, and Why He Matters* (New York, NY: HarperOne, 2011), pp. 1–2.

2. Cynthia Bourgeault. *Centering Prayer and Inner Awakening* (Lanham, MD: Cowley, 2004), p. 13.

3. Amos Smith. *Healing the Divide: Recovering Christianity's Mystic Roots* (Eugene, OR: Wipf and Stock, 2013), p. 201.

4. "God's Real Presence" is a phrase often used by Quakers. The idea is that just as Catholics and others refer to the "Real Presence of Christ" in the elements of bread and wine in Holy Communion, so too the Quakers and other refer to the Real Presence of God available in silent prayer.

5. Also known as the Alexandrian Fathers.

6. A Quaker phrase.

7. During centering prayer we experience what Gregory the Great called "resting in God."

8. In this work, Contemplative Outreach Ltd., is an excellent companion.

9. Thomas Keating. *Open Mind, Open Heart: The Contemplative Dimension of the Gospel* (New York, NY: Continuum, 2002), p. 13.

10. Ian VanHeusen. "4 Keys to Discerning God's Will," *The Art of Living Well,* July 18, 2015, https://ianvanheusen.com/4-keys-to-discerning-gods-will/.

11. Thomas Keating. *Invitation to Love: The Way of Christian Contemplation* (London, UK: Bloomsbury, 2012), p. 105. Thomas Keating was a fountainhead of Centering Prayer tradition. His organization, Contemplative Outreach, has a 300,000-member newsletter mailing list. Contemplative Outreach is a solid resource for further information on centering prayer.

12. Shunryu Suzuki. *Zen Mind, Beginner's Mind* (Boston, MA: Shambhala, 2010), p. 1.

13. Bourgeault, p. 80.

14. Maximos the Confessor. *The Philokalia*, Vol. 2.

15. The free phone app is called *Centering Prayer* in iTunes. The subtext is "Contemplative Outreach."

16. Anthony De Mello. *Awareness: Conversations with the Masters* (New York, NY: Image, 2011), p. 123.

17. The paradox for the Christian mystic is that in the absolute sense God is ultimately unknowable, yet in the relative sense, God is always knowable in the life, death, and resurrection of Christ.

18. Thomas Keating. *Manifesting God* (New York, NY: Lantern, 2005), p. 2.

19. James Finley. *Christian Meditation: Experiencing the Presence of God* (New York, NY: HarperOne, 2009), p. 17.

20. "Resting in God" is a phrase Gregory the Great (d. 604) used to summarize the essence of silent prayer. This was the classical meaning of contemplative prayer for Christianity's first sixteen centuries.

21. www.contemplativeoutreach.org.

22. Thomas Merton. *Contemplative Prayer* (New York, NY: Image, 1971), p. 67.

23. This phrase was first coined by Apollinaris of Laodicea in the fourth century, and became part of orthodoxy through Cyril of Alexandria in the fifth century.

24. I realize it is problematic to claim that God speaks to me. Sometimes people claim that God tells them to do horrible things. I think the best way to judge if God is speaking to us is to defer to the Golden Rule: "Do to others what you would

have them do to you." (Luke 6:31). If what we are hearing is contrary to the Rule, then it is not God.

25. James Finley, p. 80. (Scripture reference is based on Revelation 3:20.)

26. Basil Pennington. *Centering Prayer: Renewing an Ancient Christian Prayer Form* (New York, NY: Image, 1982), p. 78.

27. David Frenette. *The Path of Centering Prayer: Deepening Your Experience of God* (Boulder, CO: Sounds True, 2017), p. 163.

28. Evagrios was one of the Desert Fathers. This quote from his writings can be found here: http://desertfathers.blogspot.com/2011/06/works-of-evagrius-ponticuson-prayer.html.

29. Bourgeault, p. 5.

30. Throughout his journal and letters, George Fox often referred to the "Seed of Christ," which is our true self, our highest potentiality created in the Divine image.

31. Christian meditation as taught by Laurence Freeman, John Main, and the World Community of Christian Meditation.

32. http://www.contemplativeoutreach.org/category/category/lectio-divina.

33. Pennington, p. 8.

34. James Finley. *Merton's Palace of Nowhere* (Notre Dame, IN: Ave Maria Press, 2018), Kindle location 989.

35. William Menninger. "Sit Down and Be Quiet: How to Practice Contemplative Meditation," *U.S. Catholic Faith in Real Life*, https://www.uscatholic.org/articles/201311/sit-down-and-be-quiet-how-practice-contemplative-meditation-28077.

36. *Cloud of Unknowing: and the Book of Privy Counseling,* William Johnston, ed. (New York, NY: Image, 1996), p. 32.

37. Frenette, p. 172.

38. Beningus O'Rourke. *Finding Your Hidden Treasure: The Way of Silent Prayer* (Liguori, MO: Liguori, 2010), p. 154.

39. There are three types of centering-prayer practitioners, referred to in the centering-prayer community as breathers, worders, and gazers. The classic form of centering prayer is returning to a sacred word, a symbol of one's consent to God. Other common forms are returning to the breath or a sacred gaze.

40. Amos Smith. *Healing the Divide: Recovering Christianity's Mystic Roots* (Searcy, AR: Resource, 2013), p. 189

41. Richard Rohr. "Eucharist: God Is Present," *Richard Rohr's Daily Meditation,* September 25, 2014, https://myemail.constantcontact.com/Richard-Rohr-s-Meditation--God-Is-Present.html?soid=1103098668616&aid=6UQo0OHLxSg.

42. Thomas Keating is a Benedictine monk and founder of Contemplative Outreach, Ltd. He is one of the three founders of the contemporary centering prayer movement, along with Basil Pennington and William Menninger.

43. Carl J. Arico. *A Taste of Silence: A Guide to the Fundamentals of Centering Prayer* (New York, NY: Lantern, 2016), p. 157.

44. Richard Rohr. "Daily Meditation, Spirituality and the Twelve Steps (Part Two)," *Prayer and Power,* June 26, 2014, https://myemail.constant-contact.com/Richard-Rohr-s-Meditation--Prayer-and-Power.html?soid=1103098668616&aid=VM7N3TqJGCE.

45. Thomas Keating. *World Without End* (New York, NY: Bloomsbury, 2017), p. 37.

46. I now think of "saved" in a different manner. Salvation means I feel whole. In centering prayer, Jesus heals me to my innermost core. Jesus loves me and accepts me. Jesus saves me from myself.

47. Bourgeault, p. 158.

48. Here I am referring to panentheism, not to be confused with pantheism.

49. John Philip Newell. *Echo of the Soul: The Sacredness of the Human Body* (Harrisburg, PA: Morehouse, 2002), p. 61.

50. Jim Marion. *Putting On the Mind of Christ: The Inner Work of Christian Spirituality* (Charlottesville, VA: Hampton Roads, 2011), p. 226.

51. This icon, titled Christ Pantocrator, is from Saint Catherine's Monastery in Sinai, Egypt. It is the earliest representation we have of Jesus, dating back to the sixth century

52. Irwin J. Boudreaux. "Finding Your Inner Room," *A Pastor's Thoughts*, April 5, 2014, https://ijboudreaux.com/2014/04/05/finding-your-inner-room/.

53. In the sixth century the Christian mystic, Gregory the Great defined contemplation as "resting in God."

54. Quoted by Father Ron Rolheiser, "Contemplative Sound Bytes," *North Texas Catholic*, June 24, 2013, https://www.northtexascatholic.org/inspiration-article?r=XCVNKQWHG2.

55. Frank Viola and Leonard Sweet. *Jesus Manifesto: Restoring the Supremacy and Sovereignty of Christ* (Nashville, TN: Thomas Nelson, 2016), p. 72.

56. This phrase is often used by Benedictine monk and author Thomas Keating.

57. The Hebrew word ruach means wind, breath, or spirit. These terms are often used in passages referring to the Holy Spirit.

58. John O'Donohue. *Eternal Echoes: Celtic Reflections on Our Yearning to Belong* (New York, NY: HarperCollins, 2009), p. 25.

59. God did have a body during a brief period of time in an obscure province in the Roman Empire and on a speck of a planet in an average galaxy. And in another sense, we are the body of God (1 Corinthians 12:27).

60. Well-known saying of Julian of Norwich

61. John Shelby Spong. *Here I Stand: My Struggle for a Christianity of Integrity, Love, and Equality* (San Francisco, CA: HarperSanFrancisco, 2001), p. 2.

62. Tony Jones. *Did God Kill Jesus? Searching For Love in History's Most Famous Execution* (New York, NY: HarperOne, 2015), p. 167.

63. Jones, p. 170.

64. Alice Miller. *For Your Own Good* (New York, NY: Farrar Straus Giroux, 1984), p. 108.

65. Parker J. Palmer. "A Friendship, a Love, a

Rescue," *Center for Courage & Renewal*, http://
www.couragerenewal.org/parker/writings/
friendship-love-rescue/.

66. Richard Rohr. "Your True Self: You Can't
Get There . . . You Fall There," March
14, 2019, https://www.youtube.com/
watch?v=vK_lBkCyCdo.

67. Ibid.

68. Paul Coelho. *The Alchemist* (New York, NY:
HarperOne, 2015), p. 57.

69. Brennan Manning. *Abba's Child: The Cry of the
Heart for Intimate Belonging* (Colorado Springs,
CO: NavPress, 2002), p. 42.

70. Thomas Merton. *A Thomas Merton Reader* (New
York, NY: Image, 1974), p. 428.

71. I am referring to the King James Version of this
verse.

72. Robert Bly, trans. *Kabir: Ecstatic Poems* (Boston,
MA: Beacon, 2007), p. 45.

73. John Philip Newell. A *New Harmony: The Spirit,
the Earth, and the Human Soul* (San Francisco,
CA: Jossey-Bass, 2011) pp. 156–160.

74. *On Being with Krista Tippett*, "Alzheimer's and
the Spiritual Terrain of Memory," March 26,
2009.

75. Brian Zahnd. "Love Never Ends," *Clarion*, March 8, 2015, https://www.clarion-journal.com/clarion_journal_of_spirit/2015/03/love-never-ends-a-meditation-brian-zahnd-.html.

76. Phileena Heuertz. "As You Love Yourself: Where Contemplation and Action Meet," *The Table*, May 7, 2014, https://cct.biola.edu/As-you-love-yourself-contemplation-action/.

77. John Dominic Crossan. "The Character of the Christian God: The Christian Bible in the Future of Christianity," *Patheos: Progressive Christian*, September 8, 2013, https://www.patheos.com/progressive-christian/character-christian-god-john-dominic-crossan-09-09-2013.

78. Marcus Borg. *Meeting Jesus Again for the First Time: The Historical Jesus and the Heart of Contemporary Faith* (New York, NY: HarperOne, 1995), p. 135.

79. Flavius Josephus (37–100 CE) was a Roman-Jewish scholar and historian who wrote histories of the Jews and Jewish wars.

80. Professor Rufus Fears of the University of Oklahoma reiterates and affirms the statements in this paragraph in his lectures and writings. Not all Bible scholars agree with his opinions, however, and since there are no written records

of this period of Jesus' life, any narrative that we make is based purely on conjecture.

81. Robert J. Hutchinson. *The Dawn of Christianity: How God Used Simple Fishermen, Soldiers, and Prostitutes to Transform the World* (Nashville, TN: Thomas Nelson, 2017), pp. 18–19.

82. Centering prayer is about open receptivity toward any and all things that come up in prayer. Nothing is suppressed. It is allowed to run its course. Acceptance and radical inclusion are at the heart of both personal and collective transformation.

83. N. T. Wright, p. 70.

84. Richard Rohr. "The Jesus Hermeneutic," *Huff-Post*, April 7, 2013, https://www.huffpost.com/entry/the-jesus-hermeneutic_b_3641435?utm_hp_ref=religion&fbclid=IwAR3sMX78AYuG9Vk sdKjISSzEdJZnAmot9zGPsSpKgsgTvedmRXdv r4f4nWo.

85. Marcus Borg, p. 30.

86. Ibid.

87. N. T. Wright, p. 133.

88. Marcus Borg. *Jesus: A New Vision, Spirit, Culture, and the Life of Discipleship* (New York, NY: HarperOne, 1991), p. 191.

89. Ibid, p. 184.

90. Quoted in Deborah Arca, "Did God Kill Jesus? Tony Jones on the Crucifixion, Love, and Resurrection," *Patheos: Faith Forward, Progressive Christian,* March 27, 2015, https://www.patheos.com/blogs/faithforward/2015/03/did-god-kill-jesus-tony-jones-on-the-crucifixion-love-and-resurrection/.

91. Arico, chapter 3.

92. Brian McLaren. *We Make the Road by Walking: A Year-Long Quest for Spiritual Formation, Reorientation, and Activation* (Nashville, TN: Jericho, 2015), p. 118.

93. Adam Bucko and Rory McEntee. *New Monasticism: An Interspiritual Manifesto for Contemplative Living* (Ossining, NY: Orbis, 2015), p. 113.

94. Brian Zahnd. *Beauty Will Save the World: Rediscovering the Allure and Mystery of Christianity* (Lake Mary, FL: Charisma, 2012), p. 185ff. I have paraphrased Zahnd's comments.

95. Karen Armstrong. *Twelve Steps to a Compassionate Life* (New York, NY: Random, 2010). Dalai Lama. *Toward a True Kinship of Faiths: How the World's Religions Can Come Together* (New York, NY: Random, 2010).

96. Of course this is a high ideal and not always possible. Some are not capable of friendship or cooperation. But we are responsible for our own actions and attitudes, not others'.

97. Many churchgoers do not follow Jesus. They are there to experience community, exercise leadership, or because of family or societal pressure. Their central authority may be a charismatic person, a political platform, or another ideology, not Jesus.

98. Richard Rohr. "The Dualistic Mind," *Center for Contemplation and Action*, January 29, 2017, https://cac.org/the-dualistic-mind-2017-01-29/.

99. Ibid.

100. Ibid.

101. Richard Rohr. "Not Two," *Center for Contemplation and Action*, July 3, 2015, https://cac.org/not-two-2015-07-03/.

102. Marion, p. 3.

103. Ibid., p. 7.

104. Bucko and McEntee, Kindle position 2619.

105. Cynthia Bourgeault. *Encountering the Wisdom Jesus: Quickening the Kingdom of Heaven,* Audio (Boulder, CO: Sounds True, 2014).

106. N. T. Wright. *The Challenge of Jesus: Rediscovering Who Jesus Was and Is* (Downers Grove, IL: InterVarsity, 2015), p. 179.

107. Joan Chittester. "Spiritual Life Begins Within the Heart," *Awaken.org,* https://www.awakin.org/read/view.php?tid=2314.

108. Smith, Kindle location 2080.

109. Jones, p. 8.

110. All this is true when viewing God through a temporal lens. If time does not exist in eternity, however, then in one sense the Incarnation always existed, and God was always part of humanity. Jesus was the Lamb slain from before the foundation of the world (Revelation 13:8).

111. Jurgen Moltmann. *Jesus Christ for Today's World* (Minneapolis, MN: Fortress, 1995), p. 37.

112. Cyril of Alexandria. *That Christ Is One*, trans. P. E Pusey, LFC 47 (Oxford, UK: James Parker, 1881), pp.237ff.

113. Henri Nouwen. "Healing Contradictions," *Henri Nouwen Society*, https://henrinouwen.org/meditation/healing-contradictions/.

114. Christine Vaulters Paintner. *The Soul of a Pilgrim: Eight Practices for the Journey Within* (Notre Dame, IL: Sorin, 2015), p. 12.

115. Laurence Freeman. *Jesus the Teacher Within* (Norwich, UK: Hymns Ancient & Modern, 2010), p. 175.

116. Richard Rohr. "Dying to Self," *Center for Contemplation and Action*, April 6, 2016, https://cac.org/dying-to-self-2016-04-06/.

117. Brian Zahnd. "Jesus Is What God Has to Say," *Brian Zahnd*, February 12, 2015, https://brian-zahnd.com/2015/02/jesus-god-say/.

118. John 8:58.

119. Sweet and Viola, p. 40.

120. Richard Rohr. "Christ Is Everywhere," *Center for Contemplation and Action,* June 12, 2018, https://cac.org/christ-is-everywhere-2018-12-06.

121. Ilia Delio. "Universal Savior: Ilia Delio Reimagines Christ," *US Catholic*, https://www.uscatholic.org/church/2011/03/universal-savior-ilia-delio-reimagines-christ.

122. Ibid.

123. Ibid.

124. Freeman, p. 259.

125. Ilia Delio. "Confessions of a Modern Nun: The Vatican visitation prompts reflection on a religious divide," *America Magazine*, October 12, 2009, https://www.americamagazine.org/issue/710/article/confessions-modern-nun.

126. The Gospel of Thomas, Logion 77, http://www.earlychristianwritings.com/thomas/gospelthomas77.html.

127. Marion, p. 224.

128. Thomas Keating. *Manifesting God*, p. 30.

129. Cynthia Bourgeault. *Centering Prayer and Inner Awakening* (Lanham, MD: Cowley, 2004).

130. Basil Pennington. *Centering Prayer: Renewing an Ancient Christian Prayer Form* (New York, NY: Image, 1982), p. 256.

Acknowledgement

· · · · · · · · · · · · · · · · · · ·

Thank you for the many authors and teachers that taught me the power of centering prayer: Thomas Keating, Basil Pennington, Carl J. Arico, William Meninger, David Frenette, Cynthia Bourgeault, and Amos Smith. I thank Amos Smith for agreeing to write the foreword. I am grateful that Amos challenged me to write this book back in 2014. Amos is a wonderful teacher, mentor, and friend. I thank Fr. Carl J. Arico from the Contemplative Outreach for agreeing to support my book and write the foreword. I continue to learn from him and laugh as he injects his sense of humor into his work. I thank my wife, Trina, and children, Benjamin, Gabriella, and Joshua, who allowed me to escape for two to three hours at a time to write this book. I thank my editor at Anamchara Books, Ellyn Sanna, for her patience and encouragement. She was a pleasure to work with and made the process easy and enjoyable. Finally, I thank my communities at www.SilenceTeaches. com, Twitter, Instagram, and Facebook who have supported my work and with whom I continue to enjoy and learn from our dialogue.

About the Author

. . . .

RICH LEWIS is an author, speaker and coach who focuses on centering prayer as a means of inner transformation. He teaches centering prayer in both his local and virtual community and offers one-on-one coaching. He publishes a weekly meditation, book reviews, and interviews on his site, Silence Teaches.

He has published articles for a number of organizations, including Contemplative Light, Abbey of the Arts, Contemplative Outreach, EerdWord, In Search of a New Eden, the Ordinary Mystic at Patheos, and the Contemplative Writer.

Rich has been a daily practitioner of centering prayer since June 1, 2014. Centering prayer has been so life-giving and life-changing that he feels compelled to share his journey with others who wish to learn more. Rich resides with his family in Ambler, Pennsylvania. Learn more about him at www.SilenceTeaches.com.

Dante's Road

The Journey Home for the Modern Soul

Nautilus Book Awards Gold Medal Winner

This spiritual guidebook follows in the footsteps of Dante on his journey through the Divine Comedy. A fresh, modern take on this path, the book invites us to explore these questions: what is my hell and how do I move through it? What is my purgatory and what lesson do I need to take away? What is my paradise; how do I get there and how do I stay there? With wisdom distilled from the great myths, scriptures, and the world's mystics, this book is an invitation to ever-greater awakening and wholeness.

Paperback Price: $19.95

Kindle Price: $5.99

Become Fire!

Guideposts for
Interspiritual Pilgrims

Bruce Epperly invites you to join him on a holy
adventure in spiritual growth, inspired by the
evolving wisdom of Christianity and the world's
great spiritual traditions, innovative global spiritual practices, and emerging visions of reality.
By embracing the diverse insights of spiritual
wisdom givers, physicists, cosmologists, healing
practitioners, and Earth keepers, we can meet the

Earth's current
challenges with love,
joy, and a united
strength.

Paperback Price:
$24.95

Kindle Price:
$5.99

Mystic Path of Meditation

Beginning a Christ-Centered Journey

Using the Celtic tradition, David Cole explores the Christian theology that underpins meditation and discovers the practical spiritual benefits of this ancient practice.

"Meditation is one of the great treasures of our Christian contemplative tradition, though largely forgotten by modern churches. In this delightful book, David Cole gently invites readers to rediscover this ancient path to deeper relationship with God."

—Mark Kutolowski, OblSB, Salva Terra peace pilgrim and founder of New Creation Wilderness Programs

Paperback Price: $14.95

Kindle Price: $4.99

Hope in an Age of Fear

Wisdom from the
Book of Revelation

The Book of Revelation has been misunderstood as a book of future predictions and escape from the world—but it is actually a survival and transformation guide, written for people whose lives were threatened by the first-century system of domination. Kenneth McIntosh goes through the entire book, chapter by chapter, revealing Revelation's abundance of wisdom we can apply to the challenges we face in today's world.

Paperback Price:
$19.99

Kindle Price:
$4.99

Celtic Prayers & Practices

An Inner Journey

Offering simple and practical meditation techniques to deepen readers' connections with God, this book is an instruction manual for the inner journey using meditation techniques rooted in the Celtic tradition. As readers put the simple steps into practice, they will discover the Divine image that is the light in the center of their being.

Paperback Price: $12.95

Kindle Price: $4.99

www.AnamcharaBooks.com